Van Buren County
Teen Creative Writing Challenge
2018

by

William "Anthony" Bradley	Lily Griffioen
Abbey Churney	Maliah Lewnfield
Rowan Clark	Sarah Mayfield
Kylie Cox	Luz Moreno
Penny Duran	Hollie Cassandra Powless
Renee Elrod	Austin Riness
Ilona Fiedorowicz	Faith Sweet
Miriam K. Gartland	Trevor Wendt

Eric Wheeler

Cover illustration, © Ashlyn Bottger, 2018

Edited by Jeffrey Babbitt

Published through the partnership of
Hartford Public Library
Lawton Public Library
Paw Paw District Library
South Haven Memorial Library
Van Buren District Library

Printed by CreateSpace

Judges

Fiction	Cover Art	Poetry
Meghann Meeusen	Leslie	Melanie Dunbar
J.L. Panagopoulos	Helakoski	Elizabeth Kerlikowske
Elaine Stephens		Amy McInnis

Additional funding provided by
Friends of the Antwerp Sunshine Library
Friends of the Gobles Library
Friends of the Paw Paw District Library
Friends of the Van Buren District Library

Table of Contents

Preface by Jeffrey Babbitt

This year, Hartford Public Library in Hartford, Michigan, joins us! That means *every public library in Van Buren County* is represented. Our reach extends to every public school system in the county as well as to homeschoolers and students in the private schools! We have grown beyond the county borders as well. We do not limit participation by geography, mainly to make it easier on ourselves—no need to verify addresses. This year, we not only have a poet from Portage in Kalamazoo County making her *second* appearance in the Challenge, we have a fiction winner all the way from Houston, Texas! We have gone *national*, people! I think I just broke my personal rule against excessive exclamation marks.

This is a year for exclamation marks, though. This year's works strive to find richness across the spectrum of life's experiences. Our winning entries in fiction run the gamut from realistic fiction and humor to mystery, science fiction, and fantasy. We follow characters both ordinary and extraordinary: young detectives, ballerinas, orphans, students, witches, warriors, political prisoners, even personifications of Life and Death. Our winning poems explore everything from the bond between a girl and her horse and the importance of good sportsmanship to persistence in the face of mental illness and the inevitability of death.

Opening the book with an ode to books themselves, we close with a story that warns us against giving up on the light and a poem that advises us to "embrace the dark." Balance is all, and isn't this the central lesson of emerging adulthood? The next generation is getting ready to take the world into their hands. We are proud to help tell their tale.

Coverbound by Renee Elrod

A bleak, grey sky threatens rain overhead
I just can't find the will to get out of bed
Snow dusts the rooftops
I'm cold to the bone
A sharp wind that gusts
Over this dark, sad home
A sound of laughter
Is heard from afar
I see the headlights of every passing car
Everyone around me
Having the time of their lives
I'm stuck in this world
It's austere, gaunt, and lonely
For a sad someone like me
Whose expression is stony
My only escape
An adventure foretold
Bound between covers
On a shelf that is old
These stories that take me on many epic quests
With dragons, and thieves, you know the rest
A whole other universe
Unlike my own
An exploit awaits me
It just must be found
In this building of adventures
That are coverbound

Renee Elrod's "Coverbound" won Third Prize for Poetry in the Grade 9-10 category.

The Muntford Mess by Miriam K. Gartland

You've probably read about the Muntfords' missing jewels in the papers, so you might think you know how this story plays out. But newspapers like to only print what they want you to know. They tend to leave out important facts—for instance, how it was I and my sister Erin who solved the case. But that doesn't matter, because now you are going to hear the real account of how it happened.

Erin and I got dragged into the mess one sleepy Saturday morning while we were enjoying a nice cup of tea, curled up on either side of the sofa and watching our favorite telly program. There was a sharp tap on the door, clearly that of a disciplined man, and Erin went to open it. It was DCI Schmidt, one of our friends from Scotland Yard. I use the word 'friends' in the loosest of terms. I'm pretty sure Schmidt hates our guts and wishes we would vanish off the face of the planet, but I could be reading into it a little. Anyways, I was chagrined to see him standing there (and me still in my pajamas!) with his usual false smile obviously meant to annoy me. He stepped in without even waiting for an invitation and asked for a cup of tea, which I reluctantly poured.

"I think you can guess why I'm here," he said, sipping slowly. I still don't know how he manages to drink tea without getting his massive handlebar mustache wet. It defies logic.

Erin and I both nodded, and I sat up, beginning to feel excited. Schmidt only talked to us for one reason: a case.

"I need you two to take a case for me. I doubt you'll be able to handle it, but the Yard has other, more pressing, matters to attend to."

Oh, you might be wondering why Schmidt was coming to us, why he even knew we existed, in fact. About a year ago,

Erin and I became part of Scotland Yard's unofficial detective force, back when the crime wave was sweeping the city. It's a long story, for some other time.

"So, what's the case?" Erin asked, after a long pause, during which the only sound was Schmidt slowly imbibing his tea. He swallowed, smacked his lips, and waited a moment before responding.

"You may or may not have heard about it. It's the Muntford theft. Not a big case, but as of yet, there have been no significant leads.

"About a week ago, Mrs. Muntford—the widow of multi-millionaire investor Josiah Muntford, who died about a year ago—reported the theft of her most prized possession. A 24-karat gold necklace inlaid with 116 diamonds, easily worth over one million pounds. The necklace was kept in a wall safe, hidden behind one of the family portraits. Early Sunday morning, the living room window was found smashed, the safe open, and the jewelry missing. Regretfully, Mrs. Muntford but recently moved into the home, and no security measures had been taken. There were several suspects of course, but all were able to provide a sufficient alibi for the time of the crime. Oh, I like that 'time of the crime'," he said, twisting the end of his mustache into an even tighter curl. He reminded me of an extremely skinny Captain Hook. Minus the red jacket and hook, of course.

"Seems like a perfectly straightforward case," Erin said. "One of them is lying."

Schmidt widened his grin. "Exactly, doll—except, we've checked up on all of the alibis through multiple sources and each one is rock solid. Well, I've taken up enough of your time. You can start your investigations at Mrs. Muntford's current residence, 22 Sherrinford Lane. I've got to run and work on more *important* things."

He set his cup back down on the table and headed towards the door.

"Oh, and Londy?" I looked up from studying my tea and glared at him. I hate when people use the abbreviation of my name. My name is London, which just so happens to be the city in which we live. You had better use the whole thing. "You girls won't solve this one."

With that, he left, closing the door behind him.

We both just sat there, staring at the door. Erin ruffled her shoulder-length coffee brown hair and looked down at Schmidt's cup.

"Prat," she said. "He left half his tea."

"Off to Sherrinford Lane then? I know how to get there," I said, putting down my tea and getting up from the couch. I study maps of London. For fun. Erin thinks I'm insane, but I can get you anywhere in the city. She would get you lost on the way to the coffee shop.

"Of course you do," Erin replied. "But you might want to change out of your pajamas first."

* * *

The first person we interrogated was a no-go. Erin had acquired a list of the suspects from the Yard, and we set off for Sherrinford Lane. Number 22 was one of those modern marvels of architecture with so many angles and sharp edges it was a wonder you didn't cut your eyes when looking at it. The neighboring homes were less severe, but hardly.

Our first suspect was Mr. Kerr, Mrs. Muntford's neighbor on the left-hand side, who was ruled out almost entirely after we talked to him and his household for a bit. (I let Erin do all the talking. She's good at asking questions and coming to conclusions, like a legit detective. I'm more of a walking Google with an aptitude for catching clues. Yeah, she's cooler.)

Of course, we couldn't entirely rule him out, as that is almost always a fatal mistake, but we came as close as one can. He was nearly 90 years old, blind as a bat, and richer than King Midas. His alibi was flawless: he had been at a dinner party with his entire family until several hours after the crime was committed. Judging by Erin's notes, the story had been confirmed by several friends who also attended the party.

Secondly, we drilled Mr. and Mrs. Whitman, a newly married couple who neighbored Mrs. Muntford on the right side—the side of the broken living room window. At first, it seemed like they were another dead end. They couldn't keep their eyes off each other the entire time we questioned them, and I couldn't help but feel that we were very unwelcome guests. I would have written them off if it hadn't been for one thing. While Erin cross-examined them, I looked around the room sitting unnaturally straight on the couch. When a house is nearly entirely white—I mean, white tile, paint, furniture, and everything—it has that effect on you, especially if you're in jeans and a pair of trainers. I could see into their kitchen, and one of the drawers was not entirely closed, leaving the corner of a piece of paper sticking out of it.

I asked for a drink and was told to help myself to the fizzy drinks in the sizeable silvery refrigerator. I grabbed a Pepsi, though I don't particularly like it, then shifted my body a bit so that the drawer would not be visible to those in the living room. Sliding it open slowly, I peeked inside. The paper was an overdue bill, and several bounced checks lay on top of the rest of the documents inside. I slid the drawer closed again and returned to the living room, where no suspicions seemed to be aroused. I was fairly certain that Erin knew what I had been up to. When we left the Whitmans' house, I told Erin what I had seen. She frowned for a moment; it was her 'pondering' look. I could almost see her trying to connect the clues in her head, like a massive dot-to-dot of the criminal.

"It makes sense, but they had an airtight alibi. My stinking goodness, they were at their own wedding!"

"But the papers! And they're on the side of the window!"

"London," Erin warned. I hung my head. Older sisters may be a pain, but no matter how many times they mix up their facts, they usually know best, especially when your imagination begins to interfere with your logic.

"Sorry. Bending facts again. I'll stop."

"Smashing. Our last suspect is the nanny of Mrs. Muntford's child. Apparently, she's down on money, but there's no other evidence against her," Erin said, consulting her list again.

"Let me guess; she has an impeccable alibi?" I asked.

"Yep," Erin replied, popping the *p*.

"Brilliant."

We marched up the long drive of Mrs. Muntford's modern marvel, and knocked on the tinted Plexiglass door. It was opened by a young woman dressed in jeans and a button-down shirt, sharply in contrast to the stiff exterior. "What can I help you with?" she asked.

"We're the police ... sort of. We're here to ask some questions," I said. Perhaps it was my imagination, but I thought I saw the woman close the door about a half-inch. She wavered for a moment, then ushered us in.

"I'll ask Mrs. Muntford if you're allowed. Wait in the lounge until I come back," she said, showing us into what was obviously the living room, judging by the 70-inch plasma screen on the wall, the massive sofa, and the boarded-up window. Everything was white, much like the Whitmans' home. The entire room seemed to have been doused in bleach. Except for one section of the wall, on which was hung about one hundred of a child's crayon drawings.

The young woman exited, leaving Erin and me alone. Or, at least it *seemed* like we were on our own. Before we had time to say a word to each other, a curly little head popped over the edge of the sofa. The head belonged to a small boy, not more than five or six, who then scrambled over the top of the sofa and landed on the floor in a heap. He then crawled on his hands and knees over to where we were standing and looked up. "Are you good fellows or the bad ones?" he asked.

"What?" I asked.

He gestured to another corner of the room. "Over there's where the bad spies are. I've just escaped from their prison. I'm Ody."

"London," I said, shaking hands with him. "And she's Erin. She'll play spies with you."

Surprisingly, I did not get a dirty look from Erin. It may come as a shock to you, but she's much better with little children than I am. Really, she has to look after me, so she gets plenty of practice. While she and the boy played their game, I wandered about the room, hoping to pick up a clue. The boy's drawings were rather good for a child of his age, and they were most certainly colorful. Most of the drawings showed a woman with a sad face, probably his mother, Mrs. Muntford. A child's perception of grief. I could hear Ody and Erin in the background.

"But I don't see a door there," said Erin.

"No, you can't just look at what's already there, you have to step back and *really* look at it," Ody replied, trying to explain his imagination. Just then, Mrs. Muntford and the young woman returned to the room. Mrs. Muntford was much different than I expected. She didn't look to be more than half a dozen years older than Erin, and was dressed in white pants and a blue blouse. The young woman took Ody out of the room and didn't return.

"You wanted to ask me a few questions?" Mrs. Muntford's voice was melodic and soft. Erin began her usual questioning routine as I looked out the window. As I did, I caught sight of something, several somethings, actually, just below the boarded-up window. Bits of glass, glistening in the sunlight. *Outside* the window. That indicated a blow from the inside of the building.

"And your boy's nanny, do you suspect her?" Erin asked. I joined her on the sofa.

"Of course not. Esmerelda takes wonderful care of Odysseus. I would trust her with my life," Mrs. Muntford said. As I looked closer at her, Ody's drawings made more sense. There were lines about her face and mouth that suggested grief and her eyes seemed sad. Poor thing must have taken her husband's death quite hard.

"I'm sorry, did you say, Odysseus?" Erin asked, forgetting politeness for a moment. A smile flitted across Mrs. Munford's face.

"Yes, my husband loved noble Greece, its history, its art. He was the one to choose Ody's name."

"I see. Well, thank you for letting us take up so much of your time, Mrs. Muntford. We hope to be back with the answer to your puzzle soon enough," Erin said, getting up from the couch.

We left the house, just as the sun was beginning to slip below the horizon. We hailed a taxi and took the half-hour trip back home, stopping once to get Chinese take-out. Back at the flat, we reviewed the information amid the smell of eggrolls and General Tso's chicken.

"Run everything by me," Erin asked me. What did I say about walking Googles?

I started with everything Schmidt had told us, then moved on to the information about the suspects.

"Suspect Number One was a flop. Unimpeachable alibi and no apparent motive for the crime. Suspects Number Two also have an airtight alibi, but clues were found on the site (overdue bills and bounced checks) that suggest they are down on money. Suspect Number Three is supposedly down on cash, works inside the home, and would have every opportunity to commit the crime. But she has another airtight alibi. I hate perfect alibis," I said, losing my focus for a moment. \

"While we were at Mrs. Muntford's, I noticed that there were a bunch of glass shards around the outside of the window, indicating that the window was broken from inside the building. Yet another piece of evidence against Esmerelda."

Erin sighed. "We've a long night ahead of us."

* * *

Guess who called us not long after we had been home? Yep. Schmidt. And since Erin was busy doing her dot-to-dot thing, I had to talk to him.

As far as facts that I could tell Schmidt, our investigation had been a damp squib, a complete and total failure. We only had speculation, which is worth nothing when talking to someone like him. So, after 15 minutes of a phone conversation with him, I was peeved.

I picked up my notebook and sat sideways on my armchair, my legs hanging from one of the arms. I began to sketch various pictures, most of which involved Schmidt dressed as a clown or wearing a frilly red cloak and being eaten by an alligator. It elevated my mood immensely.

"You can't look at what's already there, you have to step back," Erin muttered, from where she was curled up on the sofa. I wasn't sure why she was repeating the words of a first grader and continued to sketch.

Erin shot up as fast as if a squirrel had gone down her shirt. (Not that squirrels are really notorious for doing that.)

"London, what's the insurance coverage on stolen valuables?!" she asked, breathing like she'd just swum across the Channel.

It took a moment for the meaning of her words to sink in, as I was preoccupied by drawing a feather in Schmidt's hat.

"It depends on the worth of the valuable, but it's probably around… Holy Fire and Brimstone!!!" I yelped. To the average onlooker, it would seem that another squirrel had crawled down my shirt. "We have to talk to Mrs. Muntford again."

* * *

When we confronted Mrs. Muntford, she didn't even try to deny it. She started weeping, making her mascara run. Bit by bit, we got the story out of her, in between sobs and hiccups.

After Mr. Muntford had died, his investments had begun to fail. Slowly but surely, Mrs. Muntford's financial state had deteriorated, until she was on the verge of bankruptcy. The final blow hit somewhere around three months ago when certain individuals threatened to release information about Mr. Muntford that would tarnish the Muntford name, and undoubtedly cause a nationwide scandal. Of course, I can't tell you what it was, but I will say that neither Erin nor I condemn the woman in the least.

The bankruptcy and blackmailers nearly drove Mrs. Muntford to a breakdown. And that was when she struck on it. She decided to fake a theft of her jewels to claim the insurance on them and pay off the blackmailers. Sunday was Esmerelda's day off, and Mrs. Muntford sent Ody to bed early. Then she broke the window and hid the jewels off the property. Naturally, since she reported the theft and showed all the signs of a distraught victim, no one suspected her. Except us. Well, Erin. I was too busy drawing Schmidt getting eaten by a crocodile. I never said I wasn't childish.

If I ever feel like quitting and becoming a cashier instead of a detective, I will recall the image of Schmidt's face when we told him we had solved it, and I will remember that this job does have its perks. It was priceless. Mrs. Muntford's court case is to be held in a few weeks, and I most certainly hope that the judge lets her off light.

Of course, when the official story was printed in the papers, the Gray sisters' involvement (that's Erin and I) was kept on the down-low. But now you know the real story. Erin said she gets to narrate the next story because I gave myself too much "screentime." She's probably right. My work here is done.

London out.

Miriam K. Gartland's "The Muntford Mess" won First Prize for Fiction in the Grade 7-8 category.

Searing Cold by Rowan Clark

The wooden guardians transform
Utilizing their colorful camouflage
As armor against the extreme conditions
Only to rid themselves of protection.

Why are they so easily defeated by the frigid conditions?
At first appearing a powerful brick wall
However, they are cowhearted
Purging themselves of all aggression the moment they feel the
      gelid air.

Every year shedding and growing new leaves
Producing leaves,
Only to fall yet again.
The pine trees seem wise; they keep their needles.

The cycle starts and ends with a silver wind
Whispering secrets about the past and future
About the fascinating forests
About the colorful autumn trees.

However, mostly they talk about the winter
How the leaves would dance to the ground and abandon the
      trees,
Just like the years before.
If they danced they must have been happy. If they danced they
      must have been happy.

*Rowan Clark's "Searing Cold" won Third Prize for Poetry in
the Grade 7-8 category.*

Counting Chickens by Penny Duran

It was a week before Easter and two weeks more until the performance. We didn't have much time for further rehearsals. I was sitting on the ground of the studio alone with my thoughts and leaning against the wall. I had already warmed up. As I crossed my bare arms for warmth in the drafty room, my sister "L" arrived. We sat silently leaning against each other waiting for everyone else to arrive.

After a small eternity, the rest of the girls arrived done up in leotards with tightly pulled up hair and in a wild chatter. Madame Kowalski—our ballet instructor and choreographer—hauled props in, finally making an attempt to move a stubbornly heavy wardrobe. Madame Kowalski had been all abeam when she brought the wardrobe to an earlier rehearsal, after having discovered it at an estate sale. Now, as she struggled to move her burden, the male lead came to her aid. I smiled at the interlude, happy to finally get started. I glanced at the poster of the current production, *La Fille Mal Gardée—The Wayward Daughter*. It was sloppily taped onto the mirrors, though it didn't matter much. It wasn't necessary to advertise to us.

L helped me onto my feet since, together with Angeline, we would begin the show. My chicken feet were a bit tired and stiff from resting my tail feathers, though I knew by the end of the rehearsal they would hurt even more. We stood in the center of the studio, pretending that it was the stage-turned-country-house courtyard. As soon as the music commenced, we started scurrying around like chickens, or at least in a ballet-interpreted chicken dance. We tried to be the most graceful chickens we could be until the male lead "scared us away" and off the stage. There we perched, off to the side, waiting for our turn to come again.

Our chicken scene had gone smoothly, even my turns, with which I had been having difficulties. We were all in sync, and at the moment the only thing likely to go wrong was a costume malfunction. While the opening scene was the longest of our scenes, my favorite part was still the storm scene where we chickens would briefly dash in a mad spree. Though it was short, it was an insane pleasure as we pretended to be gone with the wind.

Beyond the dancing were props and other stage handling. The director assigned who would stage which prop, and assigned me, L, and Angeline to carry the wardrobe, in which the male lead would later hide from the wayward daughter's mother. In the commotion of rehearsal, she gave us a hurried warning. The door easily gets jammed and locked and can only be opened from the outside. Giddy about the coming holiday and performance, L and I nodded in acknowledgment as we packed our bags to go home and get ready for the long holiday weekend.

Easter was quite nice. After lots of egg painting and chocolate eating, everything fell into place, and I had never felt more well rested and ready for a performance.

The day of the show, we went over *everything* in a dress rehearsal, and strangely, I wasn't the slightest bit nervous. Despite trifles such as a headpiece that was a little too small and my sore feet, I was sure that the performance would go great. After all, I could truly count on everyone, especially my fellow chickens, or *Dixie Chicks* as Dad would joke. Once we finished the dress rehearsal, we were relieved, and after a while, a little bored. And for this common problem, we struck on a simple solution: *hide and seek.*

I was designated the seeker, while Angeline, L, and a younger girl hid. Angeline was quick to find, hiding in the bathroom. Though it took some time, I eventually found the younger girl in the empty chairs for the audience. However, one person remained well hidden—L. At first I thought I had overlooked her, as I often do when I misplace things, or that she had simply found a really good hiding spot. Eventually Angeline and the little girl joined in on the search, but we couldn't find L anywhere!

"It's OK," I said more to myself than to the others, "She's just messing with us. As soon as it's show time, she'll show up. She always does."

But as it approached five PM, half an hour before the show, L was still missing.

I eventually lost composure and pleaded to Angeline, "Where is she? I'm tired of her leaving whenever she wants and doing whatever she wants without ever telling anyone! Being independent doesn't mean being selfish."

"Relax, she'll be back," Angeline comforted. "She probably had to do something. Leaving others behind isn't in her nature. Just trust me, alright?"

"Alright, I really hope you're right," I said, while silently adding, *because if I can't count on her, who can I count on?*

* * *

Ten minutes until the show and still not a trace of L. Carolina came up and asked where L was and turned glumly away when I said I didn't know. In my anxious state, I went to Madame Kowalski to tell her L was missing and that I'd looked everywhere for her.

I asked, "What should we do if she doesn't come?"

"Just improvise and do your best," she said with a smile, though I could sense her agitation for L's absence. Madame Kowalski's advice was easier said than done.

As Angeline and I stood behind the curtains, waiting for them to open, I heard her mumbling *"wecandoitwecandoit wecandoit,"* all the words melting together in one nervous chant. Regrettably, the attempt at comfort did not suffice. We no longer felt as secure as we had during the dress rehearsal. Still, when the curtains opened, we were immediately focused on the act. Besides, it is very difficult to mess up running around liked crazed chickens. The audience did not notice that we were short of a chicken. Once the male lead "chased us away," Angeline and I looked at each other and tried to communicate using only our eyes. But "talking" this way to Angeline was not the same as with L. Even though Angeline and I were great friends, L and I were sisters and had an unspoken connection.

I reluctantly went on stage for our next scene, doing a waving motion for Angeline to come as we had rehearsed. Though we had fake smiles plastered across our faces, one could easily read through our body language that something wasn't right. Some from the audience could certainly see a gaping hole where L was supposed to be standing.

Just play it cool, I told myself, *so the audience won't notice.* But maybe they already had.

As I did my *fouettes*, Angeline hopped lonesome towards the corner. I tried to remain composed. It would be over soon, and it wouldn't happen again. I planned to make sure of it. As Angeline and I held each other's backs doing a cancan sort of chicken walk, I put my hands on my hips in order not to reveal L's disappearance. When we posed for the end of our dance, I muttered under my breath: "When I get home L is so ..." but I tossed that thought away.

Our next scene—the storm scene—went well. It was as if my qualms were blown away by the imaginary winds. It was nearly as fun as it had been during rehearsals. As soon as we got backstage, I was again frustrated as I contemplated moving the heavy wardrobe onto the stage. Without L there to help, it certainly felt heavier. We could barely move it. Luckily, Carolina came and helped us.

As I looked at the show from backstage, I sighed at how it was hard to do even the simple things without L. Lost in my thoughts, I scratched at the floor with my ballet slipper turned chicken foot. My thoughts were interrupted as I heard a pounding noise from somewhere. I ignored it at first because there were so many things going on. Then I followed with my eyes as Madame Kowalski and the male lead ran toward the wardrobe to hide inside. They opened the door and something ... *yellow* ... fell out.

The lost chicken, who had succumbed to a poor choice of hiding spots, landed ungracefully on her back. She was quick on her feet and got back up in the blink of an eye. Her face was theatrical since she had been cooped up and waiting to be let out. The faces of Madame Kowalski and the male lead were anything but composed. L quickly scurried off in a mad fury, putting our run during the storm scene to shame. Yet the show went on. L and I looked at each other, speaking our optical tongue. Along with Angeline, we embraced each other, happy that L hadn't abandoned us.

We did our bows following our hysterical performance, with the audience none the wiser. The crowd clapped, and especially wildly for the comic relief chicken. As we stepped forward smiling into the crowd, most of us wore fake, exhausted smiles, but not me. Mine was sincere.

L cocked her head and gave me a perplexed look. "Critter," she asked, using her nickname for me, "why are you so happy?"

"Because I can always count on my chickens, L," I said, as my smile grew even wider.

Penny Duran's "Counting Chickens" won Third Prize for Fiction in the Grade 9-10 category.

~Isaiah~ by Sarah Mayfield

I hear a neigh through the wind
I smile as his bristly mane brushes against my face
He canters around me
And bucks with joy
Kicking up a cloud of dust
I haven't seen him in a while
So to be with him makes me smile

Sarah Mayfield's "~Isaiah~" won Second Prize for Poetry in the Grade 7-8 category.

Dangers in Cali by Luz Moreno

Arizona is where our story started.

There were three totally different girls who hated each other so much. Their names were Maria, Esperanza, and Citlali (aka Laly). Maria lived on a ranch. She had horses, cows, sheep, chickens, and all types of farm animals. She didn't really have friends. Her only friends were the people who'd go to their ranch to race their horses. Maria didn't care about others and their opinions. She would say whatever crossed her mind without thinking who it would affect.

Now for Esperanza. Well, there's not much to know about her. Esperanza was a regular girl with a regular life, or that's what she thought. Esperanza played soccer and basketball, and she was very good at the sports. During her free time, she went to the gym; to her, health was the most important thing ever. Also, Esperanza was a youth group leader at her church, to which her parents donated money every year for construction and everything the church might need.

Now, Citlali. Well, she was more different than the other girls. Laly's parents seemed to be the parents everybody wants. They seemed like a happy family, but Laly's mom found things out about her dad she didn't like. She decided to divorce him. Little did she know that was going to hit Laly really, really hard. Well, Laly started smoking and selling pot. She also started going out every weekend and partied really hard.

Now, these three girls didn't always hate each other. They actually grew up together. Their dads worked for the same company, but the girls didn't know as what. Once the girls got to middle school they started to lose connection, since they hung out with different cliques. Some rumors were going around that made them hate each other, and they were no longer were friends.

It was senior year, and Maria's parents invited Esperanza's and Laly's to their beach house in San Francisco. They thought it would be a good idea for the girls to spend time together like the old days, but the parents weren't coming along, so the girls drove in the same car. It was a really awkward trip for them.

Finally, Laly looked at Maria and Esperanza and said, "Can we make a stop?"

Maria said, "Laly, we have 20 more minutes. Can you wait?"

Laly responded, "Sure, but just know when we get there, I'm not staying at your beach house, Maria. I need my own space, so I'm staying with some people I know."

Esperanza responded, "Yeah, for what? So you can smoke and drink on your own? Probably not. We're here to spend time together, not do whatever we want."

Maria said, "Laly, grow up. We're going to have so much fun, and you'll learn to have fun without putting bad stuff in your body."

Finally, the girls got to their destination.

Maria grabbed her luggage just like the other girls did. Once the girls got inside, Maria noticed that a lot of things had changed. It was strange, because she and her family hadn't been down here in years, but she didn't mention it to the girls.

Laly said, "So, are you just going to stand there or show us our rooms?"

Maria showed the girls their rooms. Finally, after two hours of making themselves at home, Maria called the girls down to the living room.

Esperanza said, "Hey, I really appreciate you having me here. I like how there's a gym nearby. I will definitely be there a lot."

Maria replied, "Well, you're welcome, but just know we're not friends, so don't get so comfortable."

Laly said, "What do you want, Maria? I don't have time for your crap."

Maria replied, "OK, first of all, don't talk to me like that when it's *my* house. Second of all, the whole day is planned out for us starting tomorrow. First, we're going with Esperanza to the gym, then we're coming back to swim at the beach, then going shopping, then looking for stray animals, and …"

Laly interrupted, "OK, I'm not doing any of that. Maybe going swimming, but I'm not going to look for stray animals. Maria, you have to take our opinions into consideration, too. Not everything is about you."

Maria replied, "Don't worry, hun. Esperanza and I decided this is what we want to do."

Esperanza sighed, and Laly replied, "Yeah, but I'm here, too. You should have asked me."

Esperanza said, "Look, Laly. All you do is party and do drugs. You need to do different things, OK, sweety?"

Maria continued, "Anyways, like I was saying, after we look for stray animals, we'll go to a beach party. So, yes, I did think of you, Laly."

The next day the girls did everything they said, and it was time for the party.

Esperanza said, "What am I supposed to wear to these things? A dress?"

Maria replied, "No, silly. Wear shorts and a shirt."

Laly said, "Hurry, guys! We're going to be late!"

Twenty minutes later, the girls had arrived at the beach party. They didn't know who was hosting it, but it's not like it mattered, right? Once the girls got there, Maria met a guy named Max, Esperanza met a guy named Daniel, and Laly … well, Laly was gone, but the girls didn't realize it.

Meanwhile, Laly was inside the big beach house. There, she discovered something that was going to change the girls lives completely.

The party was finally over, and Maria and Esperanza went back to the house. The girls didn't think too much of Laly not being there, because they knew how much of a party animal she was. They thought she would find her way back.

The next morning, Esperanza said, "Dude, I feel like we should look for Laly. She isn't home.

Maria replied, "She's fine. You know how she is. It isn't such a big deal."

But Esperanza said, "Maria, we're in a whole different state. It matters. Plus, if we don't look for her, then I'll just call the cops."

Before Maria could respond, the doorbell rang. She went to open it, but nobody was there.

Before she could close it, Esperanza said, "Look! There's a letter down on the rug. Get it!"

Maria got the letter and went back to the kitchen. The girls opened the letter and read:
If you want your friend Citlali back go back to the beach at midnight alone with no cops.

Esperanza was so in shock she started crying and wanted to call the cops, but Maria didn't let her.

* * *

Meanwhile, Citlali was roaming the streets of San Francisco trying to find out how to tell the girls what she had found out. Laly didn't sleep at all the night before. She was too much in shock and now sort of depressed. She finally realized why her life was the way it was, why everything was so easy for her family, and why her parents would send her away often. Laly stopped by a taco truck to get some tacos. There she saw a group of people that looked somewhat like they belonged in the streets.

She went to them and said, "What's up?"

One girl turned, looked her up and down, and said, "What do you want?"

Laly replied, "Can I not say 'What's up'?"

The girl said, "Don't get smart with me. I said, 'What do you want?'"

"Yeah, and I said, 'What's up,' so *what's up?*"

"What's your problem?"

"No, what's *your* problem?"

The girl and her "crew" got irritated. The girl tried to punch Laly, but Laly kept dodging the hits and threw the girl to the floor. The whole crew was shaken, including the girl.

Finally, the girl got up and said, "I like you. What's your name?"

Laly, already knowing what she knew, couldn't risk letting people know who she was—including these people. So she responded, "L."

The girl replied, "L? Well, my name is Stacey, and this is Leo, Vianney, Stephanie, Emilio, Fernando, Lexis, and Kevin."

The nine of them hung out the whole day. They told Laly how they didn't have families, how they were each other's family, and they did graffiti for a living.

Kevin said, "Look, L, this is some of our work." The work was so beautiful, but Laly knew that the work came from poverty and the real struggles of people.

* * *

Midnight came around. Maria and Esperanza got tasers and went to the beach to get Citlali back. The girls waited half an hour at the beach, and they were very scared.

Esperanza said, "What if this is one of her jokes?"

Maria replied, "First of all, Laly doesn't do jokes. Let's just wait 10 more minutes. If she doesn't show up, we're calling the cops."

Five minutes went by, and the girls were very anxious. They saw two shadows coming toward them. Esperanza pulled out her taser. It was Max and Daniel

Maria asked, "What are you guys doing here?!"

Max said, "This is part of our property, and we just came for a walk. What are you doing here?"

Esperanza replied, "It's a long story, but have you seen my other friend?"

Max said, "No? Who's that?"

Maria replied, "The one who came with us to your party. We got a letter to meet someone here so we could get our friend back."

Daniel asked, "Well, did you guys bring money or any of that?"

Maria said, "No, but we br ..."

Esperanza hit Maria with her shoulder to tell her she was saying too much and said, "We brought her picture so we could look around for her."

Max replied, "Oh, OK. Well, why don't you guys come with us? It's late out here, and I don't think the person you're waiting for is going to show up."

Esperanza said, "No, it's fine. We'll go back home."

Maria said, "Are you kidding me? I'm scared to even be here! Let's go with them."

The four of them walked to Max's car and drove past the city and into a rural area.

Once they got to their destination, Max brought the girls inside his cabin and said, "You guys will be safe here from whoever is trying to harm you and your friend Citlali."

Esperanza replied, "OK. Are you guys going to stay with us?"

Daniel said, "No. We have to go back to the city for work and then go to the beach to make sure everything is going fine. We'll be back in two days."

Once the guys left, the girls went to their room and noticed there were clothes there, as if this was planned out.

Esperanza said, "This is getting really weird, and I don't like it. I think we should call our parents."

Maria said, "How is it weird? And no, we can't call our parents! What are we going to tell them, 'Oh we lost Laly'?"

Esperanza replied, "It's weird because, first of all, we never said Laly's name, but they knew her. Plus, we never call Laly Citlali, *but they knew her first name!*"

Maria said, "OK, this *is* weird. Let's call our parents."

The girls looked for their phones and realized they had left them in the car. Esperanza told Maria they should get out, but they knew they were no longer in San Francisco. They didn't know their way back, so they both agreed to wait and play along.

* * *

Stacey and Leo showed Laly all the places they stayed.

Leo said, "We don't all stay together. We get separated in groups of two. Me and Stacey always stick together, but now that there's an odd number of us, you're welcome to stay with us."

Stacey looked Laly up and down and said, "You don't have a family, do you?"

Laly replied, "No. My parents died six months ago, and I've just been taking care of myself ever since. They wanted to put me in a foster home, so i ran away, because I can take care of myself."

Leo said, "How have you been doing it? Like taking care of yourself? On your own?"

Laly said, "I don't know. I've been through a lot. I guess it's just luck."

Then, night came around. Laly was sleeping while Leo and Stacey were packing their stuff to meet up with the others.

Leo said, "I'm kind of liking the girl. Too bad we have to do this."

Stacey replied, "Yeah, me too. But we can't just back out now. It's too dangerous. Plus, there's a lot against us."

Leo woke up Laly to tell her to get ready because they were going to meet up with the others.

"We'll be in the van," he said. "You have 10 minutes."

Laly got up and ran through the back door. She had heard enough to know what was going on. She ran through some buildings. Two guys stopped her and asked her what was wrong. Laly just said she was going for a run.

One of the guys said, "It seems more like you're running away from something. Is everything OK?"

Laly replied, "Yes, I'm sure. Can I just get my workout over with?"

The other guy said, "What's your name? Mine's Max."

Laly turned around, told them to mind their own business, and kept running. Max and Daniel looked at each other and ran after her.

Once they caught up to her, Daniel grabbed Laly and said, "We know who you are, and you're coming with us."

Laly begged them to let her go, but they didn't. Once they got in the car and drove off, Laly recognized Esperanza's and Maria's phones on the floor. She picked them up and hid them.

Daniel and Max dropped off Laly at a house and threw her inside. Once they left, Maria and Esperanza saw her.

Maria yelled, *"Citlali, where have you been?"*

Laly told them everything. They decided to call their parents, tell them what was going on, and ask them to come for them at Maria's parents' beach house.

Laly grabbed a vase and threw it at the window. A loud alarm went off. Before they could all get out, cops surrounded the house. They finally ran away from the house.

A cop pulled out his phone and called someone, saying "They're gone."

The girls ran as fast as they could and finally got to the city. They ordered a cab and asked the driver to take them to the beach house. Once the girls got to their destination, they saw their parents.

Laly said, "We have to ask you something."

They all paid attention and Laly told them everything they found out and everything they been through in less than a week.

Laly's dad looked at her and explained to her that they were all undercover agents trying to arrest someone back home. That's why they sent them away. A lot of people knew who they were and how their dads were agents, so they wanted to harm them. After that, they all went home amazed at what they heard.

A couple of hours later, Max and Daniel's crew were arrested and sent to jail.

Luz Moreno's "Dangers in Cali" won Second Prize for Fiction in the Grade 11-12 category.

Untitled prose poem by Maliah Lewnfield

His palms were sweaty, his hair was crazy, and he smelt of a strong cologne scent. Every time I heard his voice, it was like waves crashing together. But the sound of the waves always put me at ease. He was like flowers in my lungs, beautiful, but I could barely breathe. Now that he was gone, the air was stale, and when I breathed it in my body, I coughed. I felt like I was stuck in time because everything was turning black and white. I could no longer see color.

Maliah Lewnfield's untitled prose poem won First Prize for Poetry in the Grade 9-10 category.

Spirits Bond by Eric Wheeler

My fingers find the spaces in between Liam's. His hand is soft, but strong, very much like the rest of him. I look up into his emerald eyes. His dark brown hair curls around his forehead. His shoulders are wide and muscular. An ideal boyfriend, but like Romeo, I am not supposed to love him.

"Liam, what are we gonna do?" I ask him, as his fingers rub against my knuckles. He looks down at my hand, in deep concentration. It is another reason I love him. He is just so adorable, the way he overthinks everything. The way he tries to help so many people.

Then again, I am pretty sure we are meant to be together. The silver cord that seems to tie us together makes me think so. It is invisible to other people, but to us, it is clear. I don't know if people can really be "soulmates," but it seems real enough for us.

"Vera, we can run," Liam says. I bite my lip, a nasty habit of mine.

Of course we could run, but what would we leave behind us? Would the covens actually strike each other? Would they openly attack each other? What would Karen think of her?

"No, we can't," I begin. "They could use our absence as an excuse to attack each other."

The night scent of the forest surrounds me.

Could we stop it? In Romeo and Juliet *they tried to use their love to end their families' grudge. Could we do the same with our covens?*

"We can't do this anymore," Liam says and stares into Vera's eyes. "*I* can't do this anymore. Having to meet you in secret, always keeping it a secret. We …"

"Vera!" A shout cuts across the empty sky. The voice belongs to a woman known as Jessica—second in line to become the High Priestess of my coven, the Moonlight Coven.

A sigh slips through Liam's lips. He gives me a curt nod and presses his lips into my forehead. He stands and walks off into the forest. It is the only thing that physically keeps us and the covens apart. Well, and now the fog that is rolling in. I turn and stride toward the Moonlight Coven's home.

Jessica is waiting for me at the doorstep. She is a plump woman with long auburn hair. She has dark, piercing eyes, and at the moment they look menacing. She stands with her hands on her hips and her lips pursed together in a thin line.

"Where have *you* been?" Her voice rises on me. I open my mouth to explain why I was not here, but another voice pierces the air with a melodic tune.

"Jessica, Vera is not restricted to the house and has full right to move around. I assure you that she was probably enjoying the moon's gaze under a beautiful sky." Karen strides forward from the home. She is by far the most elegant woman Vera has ever seen.

Karen's golden hair falls upon her shoulders and passes down to to the middle of her back. Her beautiful blue eyes seem to pass every mental defense and see into my soul. She is naturally pale, but her skin seems to glitter with energy when she steps out of the home. Karen wears her pale peach color ceremonial dress. It drapes over her shoulders and is naturally tight on her thin body, allowing the onlooker to see every detail. The dress also allows her much movement, and the split at her legs allows for running.

"Come in, Vera. Let's get you out of the coldness of the night so we may start our prayers," Karen says, gesturing a friendly hand toward the door. Jessica is already in.

I walk up into the house, heat radiating onto my skin instantly. The first room is the living room. Two couches and a small love seat fit the place around the coffee table. A large flat screen television hangs from the left wall, with a hallway to its left. To my right, another hallway leads off to our dining room and kitchen. A soft glow emits from a few candles stationed around the room.

Jessica already sits in one of the chairs, and the other members of the Moonlight Coven help themselves to seats. Some glance up at me, but the others mind their business.

I slowly find my way to a chair that is neglected. With amusement, I watch the other witches of the coven speak about spells and other witchy things so openly. I am in the debt of them all. They accept me as part of their coven, and here I am, trying to break their rules by seeing Liam. I bite my lip again.

The room falls with a silence that would be awkward, if there weren't a goddess in the front of it. Karen stands in front of their group, her white teeth showing. Power seems to glow from her. She elegantly walks forward, her arms spreading forward to motion to everyone.

"For our holiday, Beltane, we will welcome our newest witch into our ranks. Vera, please stand," Karen says.

I look across the room at all the witches. All of them are a picture of beauty, and their robes make them look much older and more powerful. My eyes land on Karen's and she gives me a courageous smile and nod.

Like a disease infecting others, her smile melts onto my face, and I begin to stand. The witches start to clap, and some whistle. Their faces go from curiosity to joy, except for Jessica. Karen then reaches her hands toward the sky, her beautiful body emphasized by the candle light. My eyes shift as I see other witches doing the same thing.

Karen's hands come down around her neck and she removes the amethyst necklace that hangs there. She steps forward, bringing the necklace around my neck. It is cold but also very welcoming and seems to have a buzz to it—or is that my breathing?

"Thank you," I whisper, a never ending smile upon my face. For a moment there is a change in Karen's expression. Her eyes unfocus and refocus, her face dropping and coming back together in a mere second.

"Vera, you are the key. Never forget that," Karen says. And then, with another unfocusing, she smiles again, her words lost.

"What do you mean Karen?" I ask, confusion bubbling in me. *Key?* Karen raises her eyebrow and that is evidence enough that I have lost my mind. I smile and wave my hand away from the topic.

"Now let's enjoy this delicious-looking food!" Karen says, clapping her hands together and eyeing the food that sits on the dining table in the other room.

* * *

Five days ago ... I take a deep breath of the flowers and bakery smell from around the square. Cars pass by, and have to try to avoid hitting the many pedestrians. There is a constant buzz of families talking and vendors selling to customers.

I wrap my fingers around a rose, and the scent of it washes over me. Roses are a powerful symbol for love and devotion. It is sad that people use it so often, wasting its meaning. They are powerful though.

Perfect for love potions. *I let out a giggle with the thought. Even as a new witch, I know a few things. A shadow covers the flowers that I am looking at. I twirl around to come face to face with a man. He is tall, with wide, muscular shoulders. His eyes watch me; dark curls surround his face.*

I raise my hand to wave. I freeze up. A silver cord that buzzes connects my hand and his chest. No, not just his chest— his heart. I look up at him and I know who he is.

Liam.

With the single thought, he smiles at me.

* * *

Present, later that night ... I drop from the roof onto the ground, dashing into the ever-growing mist. The mist crawls into wisps around my legs as I run. The air around me ripples with each step. He is close. The vibration in the air ripples more. Then, with a clash, I slam into a hard figure. Hands catch me before I get far.

I stare into Liam's eyes, then our lips meet. The air around us seems to buckle and almost glow around them, the energy rich. Even the mist seems to swirl around us.

"I missed you," I say after we are done. My head rests on his chest, listening to his breath and heart.

"I missed you too," Liam says after a moment. The energy around us ripples again. I blink as I reach out. My hand instantly starts to feel warm, and the mist swirls in between my fingertips. I am about to call Liam when a shout pierces the air.

I look up at Liam, his face toward the north. Then, the ground shakes, and there are more shouts. I finally recognize one—a beautiful, melodic voice that speaks in a different language. It is strange, but with every word, she gives off power. Karen's voice is not the only one. Others cut through the air.

The air around them buzzes with energy and the mists move toward the north. Butterflies fill my stomach, and a hard truth presses into my mind.

Did they find out that I left? Are the covens fighting?

I look up into Liam's eyes, but he is looking into the mists toward the north.

Karen!

I split myself from Liam and run into the mists. I can't see much except for the glow of mists. I hear another shout to my left. I run toward the shout. I see a glow of colors, and I burst from the mist.

The mists swirl around the edge of the two opposing groups. To my right, Karen has runes and symbols floating around her, all emitting different colors. She stands with pride and her usual glow of power. Her eyes fix on the Midnight Coven's leader.

The woman that Karen stares at is remarkably similar to Karen. Her body is draped with a very similar ceremonial dress, except for the mix of black and purple. Her hair flows down her shoulders, a pitch black color. Her eyes are a dark, menacing type. Her skin matches Karen's pale color. Even their faces almost match.

Mia, High Priestess of the Midnight Coven.

"Sister Karen, you know this will not end well for us," Mia says, her voice dripping with a threat. Mia also has runes floating around, but she also has a see-through barrier that surrounds her and two other witches to her right. The rest of the Midnight Coven witches are exposed but ready to fight.

Jessica steps forward and with one swift movement of her hand, a glowing whip forms around her hand and extends six feet into the air. She flicks her hand forward, the whip flying the through the air.

"No!" I shout.

The energy around me quickly fills me and I shove it out. With a bright light the energy spins through the air, hitting the whip and dissipating it. A painful silence falls over everyone. They all watch me. I look at my hands. They glow with the energy around me. A buzz of power now thumps and radiates heat; mists surround me.

Someone else's hand wraps around mine. I watch Liam as he stares at the two covens. He also glows with energy and the mists. I open my mouth, and then I close it.

"We must not kill our own kind. Witches have been together for years, and now we use our powers to kill each other. How does that make you feel?"

The voice is mine, but the words are not. They stand in shock.

"Love can be hard to find," Liam's voice echoes across the clearing. "But it is possible, if you would just stop fighting. Competing against each other. A new threat is here, and I promise that it's not each other. Love can be seen, and these two understand it,"

The mists are picking up speed, and instead of being afraid, I feel welcome.

Shouts come from the locals. I want to help, but I can't move. I struggle against the mental hold on me.

Vera, I want to say thank you. You have given these two covens a chance to live. They have a threat greater than either of them. Now it is time to come back home.

The mists cloud my view and then my mind. I fight against it. I need to tell Karen thank you. I need to tell Liam that I love him. I need to do so much. A single squeeze comes from Liam's hand. A single gesture that holds more words than even a painting.

I love you Liam.

I let go.

Eric Wheeler's "Spirits Bond" won Second Prize for Fiction in the Grade 9-10 Category.

Two Little Marks by Austin Riness

Two little marks
A universal message
"I survived
And you can too"

Two little marks
Their meaning heavy
Hard to carry
Impossible to forget

Two little marks
A peaceful protest
"We are here,
We are going to stay"

The semicolon
Holds one dear to me
Preserving her memory
Within the ink on my wrist

Austin Riness's "Two Little Marks" won Third Prize for Poetry in the Grade 11-12 category.

The Moonsword: A Tale of Two Minds and One Blade
by Ilona Fiedorowicz

Grey clouds moving in from the east looked a faded red in the yellow sky, with the sun out of sight, but still shining. Any trace of the day was only shown on the waves of the sea, as they bounded among each other. If the sky was radiant, then the waves were more so, cutting up the reflection as they did. Peace in this world was yet to spark with the twilight's captive glow.

There was a disturbance in the waves, though, as if they had been sliced through with a knife. The wake of a small ship surged through them, eventually connecting sea and ship. The *Moonwind* was a regular sight there, and a regular sight of the sea.

Atop its wood-paneled deck stood Temlok, an ambitious young man being trained in magic. His curly brown hair contrasted fiercely with his sharp green eyes, and his nose jutted off of his face like a cliff. His beard grew from his chin to his mouth about an inch across, and continued off in either direction only at the very bottom of his face, coming two inches away from his pointed ears. He was wearing a dark blue tunic, strapped around the waist with a black belt. There was no need for a coat today; the warm sea breeze called for short sleeves. Neither he nor anyone else had understood it, but he had huge hands and long fingers, so he could touch his small finger with his thumb from around his wrist. His brown trousers were tucked neatly into his sleek, dark brown traveling boots (he being the only member of the crew in shoes).

He could see stars start to peek through the clouded veil of twilight and took out his spyglass to inspect them.

Temlok had always found himself fascinated with how the water showed the stars when he looked down.

Suddenly, something shoved the telescope out of his hands and covered his eyes.

Quickly, he reached into his pocket and grasped the chain attached to a small blue stone. It heated his hand when he touched it, and its power filled him. He used it to see through the thing covering his eyes and whipped around. Standing in front of him and chuckling with amusement stood his master, Beanor.

Temlok's hand recognized the feel of the triangular-brimmed hat and the falcon feather stuck in it. It was *his* hat, of course, and he rarely went anywhere without it. Tonight, it seemed, was an exception. His hand came up and thrust the hat off of his eyes, onto his head.

"Master!" Temlok said. "I ... well ... I didn't expect your coming! Tonight I simply wished to watch the stars!"

Beanor's chuckle cut him off. "You might have known my presence if you wore that jewel around your neck as I have previously instructed! Now," he continued. "It's time for your theoretical lessons, and then off to bed!"

Temlok picked up his spyglass, closed it, and strapped it to his belt. Then, he carefully adjusted his hat. He looked down at the table Beanor was setting up in front of him. There was an old map of the sea and the islands of Ghans. Cartographers on the ship hadn't ever been anywhere outside of the sea and the islands, so the three Hindagoian landmasses were missing. Temlok was able to point out where they should have been, due to his travels and lessons from Beanor, but now his eyes were drawn to an odd drawing pictured on the map. It featured a sea serpent, a monstrous figure, twisting and coiling around a sword. Above it was drawn a circle and an arrow pointing to the sword.

"Master?" Temlok said, looking up finally from the drawing. "Do you know what this is?" He gestured to the map.

Beanor raised his eyebrows, studying it skeptically.

Finally, he answered, "That is a map, boy."

Temlok sighed, and pointed to the serpent drawing. "Yes, of course!" he said hurriedly. "I meant this! The serpent?"

Beanor pushed the map off to the side, saying only, "A lesson for another time, Temlok."

Temlok adjusted the hat on his head and scrubbed his long fingers over his beard.

"Yes," he said through his hands. "But what is the lesson for this time?"

Beanor's answer was familiar to Temlok's ears. "In due time, you shall see."

* * *

Temlok's hands reached back and grasped the cylindrical form of the scrolled map from its hiding place inside of his pocket. Tonight he would research it with the old copy of *Glyphs and Symbols* that he had in his chamber. But for now, he was making his way over toward the navigator, Digor.

"Digor!" he said as he made it to the mast. He could see the straight midnight-black hair of his friend. Digor was wearing a simple white tunic tonight with rolled up sleeves, wrapped with a brown belt. His trousers were brown and hanging loose around his bare feet, like the rest of the crew. He never wore a hat, a fact Temlok refused to understand, so his pointed ears were visible as they peaked from under his hair.

When his name was called, Digor whipped around, eyes alight in the dark moonshine of night. "Tern!" he called, using the nickname he had given Temlok. "I've been wondering what you were doing all that time! One of old Beanor's history lectures again?"

Temlok nodded. "Yes," he said. "Today's was about how the red jewel was mined, and even though I know it was the cause of all evil in this land, it wasn't the most interesting thing ever to hear about."

Digor chuckled lightly, and then Temlok's hand reached back toward his pocket as he fiercely grasped something. Temlok realized he was grasping the map and reluctantly pulled it out as to not make a fool of himself.

"So," Digor said lightly, "what's in there?"

Temlok only shrugged and unrolled his scrolled map. He pointed to serpent coiling around the sword.

"I don't have any clue what this could be, and I'm going to look in on it tonight with the old glyph book that Master gave me." He glanced at Digor, who was focused very intently on the map. "Hey," said Temlok. "What's with you?"

Digor blushed furiously, which surprised Temlok, but also let him know that whatever Digor was hiding happened to be very interesting.

"*The light in your eyes is my moonlight, it's always there in dark times*," he said in a near whisper. His voice was stronger when he next spoke. "It's Senda."

"Were you saying my name, Digor?" said Senda, revealing herself from behind the tall form of Digor.

Digor looked one last time at Temlok, and then switched his gaze back to Senda and said to her, "Captain, I need to talk to you about where we're headed. By this course we ..."

* * *

Temlok was already on his way back to the barracks for his own section. He wouldn't call the cot hanging from the ceiling a bed, because he always slept on the deck, but he kept all of his things under it. He shuffled through the papers, spyglass, books, and an odd assortment of different utensils, until he found the leatherbound five-inch thick translations book he had been looking for.

The light in your eyes is my moonlight ... moonwind ... serpent ... circle ... sword ...

Tonight was one to remember—that was sure. Right now the mysterious map was occupying most of his mind, though he also thought of his encounter with Digor. He shifted his gaze to the map once more, and something clicked in his mind. He hurried out the *Glyphs and Symbols* volume from under his bedroll, and opened to the moon page. On it, thousands of symbols from 20 different written languages (in Hindago, all spoke the same language, but wrote in many different ways). His eyes caught one picture, just a plain circle labeled *Moon, in Agonin.* Agonin was an ancient written language used only for prophecies and hidden items.

Temlok noted the sidebar, flipping to the correct page. His eyes caught on the center word. *Moonsword.* He quickly flipped several pages and found a drawing that made his heart stop. It showed the curved blade, and the serpent coiling around it. He switched his eyes to the text and whispered the words that would change his life.

"The ancient texts say the Moonsword is a sword that can kill the worst and most feared enemies known to man. This symbol depicts a serpent twisting around the Moonsword, the serpent being known as 'The Barrier Fangs'. Prophecy states that one sailor born in this century will be able to wield the sword and slay the beast with the help of an elder mind."

Temlok stared at the page in utter disbelief and re-read it three more times to make clear its meaning. He didn't know why, and certainly didn't believe it, but he had the strangest inkling of a notion that he was the sailor spoken of, and that Beanor was the "elder mind."

He promptly shut the book and gazed up at the moon. Everything in Hindago was based around the moon these days, it seemed.

* * *

"Monster! An attack on the port side! Monster!"

Temlok shot out of his bedroll. He didn't know how long he'd been asleep, but thought at this point, it must be midnight. He picked up the small jewel and clasped it around his neck, quickly creating a sword and a shield out of the magic. He rushed valiantly over to the port side, raising them up, when he saw a gleaming form beside him.

The moonlight's gleam reflected off of a perfectly tempered blade, silver-white in the night. It was perfectly curved at the end, so Temlok knew at once that he had come face to face with the Moonsword of legend. The very thing that had preoccupied his mind for the whole night was right in front of him, and all he had to do was reach out.

As he released the sword and shield from their short time in existence, his hand stretched out toward the Moonsword, his long fingers stretching beyond normal human ability. Finally, his fingers clasped around it, and he pulled with both hands.

Beanor's voice came out from across the commotion of the attack: *"Temlok! Don't—You're not ready! Temlok!"* His bare feet pounded on the wooden deck as he shot to Temlok frantically. His old, gnarled hands pushed Temlok's right hand away from the hilt.

Digor was running up to Temlok, too, saying something about an ancient force, and Senda behind him snarled in the serpent's direction.

There was a bright flash of light and a tremendous bolt from the sky. Digor fell down, blinded, and Senda caught him. After making sure he wouldn't roll off of the deck in the waves, she looked in front of her to see a smoking spot on an uncharred patch of wood right where Beanor and Temlok had been crouching.

* * *

"I told you, the red always goes first!" said Temlok, exasperated after an hour's worth of puzzles in the cave the Moonsword had whisked them to, with still no sign of the sword.

"Does this appear to be a normal situation?" Beanor's voice replied in a brisk tone.

"By your standards, apparently! How am I supposed to know you're telling the truth?"

"Ahh ..." Beanor paused in his arranging of jewels, and closed his eyes. "Notice telling *a* lie, and telling *the* truth. Almost as if ... no, not as if ..." He opened his eyes, and their piercing blue glare seemed to go straight through Temlok. "There is only one truth, and many lies. Many grains of sand, and one shaving of pure gold. There are many ways to choose, and the true is always the hardest to find, and the hardest to give. Remember that, boy. You may need it in your strive for glory here."

Temlok stared at him blankly. He blinked several times in confusion, and then spurred into a whirl of anger.

"W-what? The truth! Do you even know what I'm doing? ... Bloody ..." He threw himself on the ground, and lay there for minute on minute. His body shuddered, and he rolled over to face Beanor.

"You know ..." Temlok said, "I think I rather know what we're supposed to do. Just ... Why can't you speak straightly?" He paused, and spoke again, "I know the truth of this treacherous world! To defeat it, I will use the Moonsword!"

He turned to face Beanor, whose face was plastered with a look of confusion.

"I don't think ..." Beanor started to say.

But then, the sword drifted down from the sky and made its way into Temlok's waiting hands.

When he held it, he felt a new power surge through him, a power unlike that of the blue jewel around his neck. It was a mystery to him, surely, but he held the sword with purpose. He felt compelled to do things that he had never imagined were possible. But most of all, he wanted, with a desire beyond any he had felt, to slay the mighty Barrier Fangs. He could feel it now: how his power would slice through the bones like jelly, the form crumpling beneath his raised arms, his mouth twisted in a mighty howl of rage ... and triumph.

Then he let go.

With a great force of effort, he stopped using the power in the sword and simply held it, as an object is meant to be held.

"Beanor!" he said, his eyes glowing like embers. "We ride!"

* * *

"Digor!" came Temlok's voice. "It'll be okay! I'm going to kill the monster!"

Digor's voice was barely audible as he spoke. "Then I'm going to be okay, I guess."

"No. You may guess, but is it an educated guess? A true guess, my friend, is nothing more than words thrown in the air to keep investigation alive. So, you guess? But truly? Do you guess ... and do you believe?"

Digor lifted his hands desperately, and searched for Temlok with blind eyes. He felt Temlok's large hands, and then his arms and chest, then pointed his blind gaze in the direction of Temlok's head. His eyes shone in the moonlight with brilliance, and he smiled at his friend.

"I do believe," he said. "Go, Tern! Go! Ride the moonlight! Ride!"

Temlok raised the Moonsword so its reflective glint shone across the ship.

"The time has come that we will fear no more! We have been killed, pillaged, and burned for years by this dauntless foe! Can no one finally defeat this foe ... until today, that is? No, today, a new light shines on the small world of sailors, and the world feels small with our power. Look to me! This sword represents the light we fight for! Rise with me, and ride the moonlight!"

He pointed the sword forward, at the serpent still ravaging the sea next to them.

"We ride."

A great cry rose up from the people around him. They gathered behind Temlok and Beanor triumphantly and waited for the battle that was about to take place.

Temlok ran up to the serpent and jumped upon the great beast with the sword flashing. He swung at it, but the serpent's head came up, and at the last moment, a fang caught the deadly blade. Temlok attempted to swing it into the maw of the creature but slipped off of its back and caught the side of the boat with one hand. Holding on with hand and foot, he swung with his right hand and blocked every head-on attack with the Moonsword. He knew eventually his left hand would give away from where it was clinging, and turned around with his back facing the serpent.

He climbed up the rigging on the hull as fast as he could and ran upon the deck.

"RAAHHHHWRRR!" the serpent hissed. Temlok sprang onto its back again, the sword pointing down in such a way that he could not miss his target. When he made contact, blood began oozing from the wound in the serpent's side. It spun at him in a fury, and before he knew it, Temlok was upside down in the churning ocean. The only thing keeping him from drifting away was the Moonsword, stuck in the serpent's side.

He kicked at the beast and hammered it with his left fist, but it was a creature of the sea, and as Temlok was not, it kept him there in morbid glee.

Suddenly, the Moonsword started glowing and it forced its way all the way through the serpent. Temlok let go of it just as his hand was about to enter the body through a large grotesque hole that had appeared. He swam from under it, blood polluting his already clouded vision. He broke the surface triumphantly and gulped in the life-giving air of the warm night. He raised up his right hand to wave at the boat full of people, who were cheering for him raucously, and the sword flew from behind him. He raised his hand higher in just the right time and caught it, then stabbed backward from above his head, all the while treading water.

He caught the serpent in its head, just as it was rearing up like he knew that it was. With a triumphant twist, he slew the great beast, and its years of terrorizing and ravaging were ended, as the Moonsword's majestic form shined in the dim night.

"We did it!" said Beanor from the boat. Temlok smiled as hands pulled him upward onto the boat. Even as he lay next to Digor, with Senda above him, he knew this was only the start of what he would contribute to this world.

"We ride ... to the moonlight! For the rest of time."

Pronunciation Guide

Beanor bay-AH-nohr
Digor DEE-gohr
Senda sehn-DAH
Temlok TEHM-lock

Ilona Fiedorowicz's "The Moonsword" won Third Prize for Fiction in the Grade 7-8 category.

Wrestling by William "Anthony" Bradley

Aggressive on the mat
Builds your character
Catch your opponent in his/her mistakes
Dominating everyone you go against
Endurance can win you a match
Feeling sore after a tough meet
Gold medals make you know you've won
Hand getting raised
It hurts to lose
Just never give up
Know you're going to win
Learn from your mistakes
Motivate yourself to be the best
Never give up no matter how good your opponent is
Overcome your biggest obstacles
Push yourself until the final whistle
Quitting is letting everyone including yourself down
Red ankle band is the lucky color
Sportsmanship is the key
Takedowns lead to victories
Underdogs look good after a win
Vicious on the mat but friendly off the mat
Winning is regular
eXtra effort beats talent
You never stop moving
Zero points for your opponents

William "Anthony" Bradley's "Wrestling" won First Prize for Poetry in the Grade 7-8 category.

A Wall Between Worlds by Trevor Wendt

The hangar—submerged by the shade of tar—loomed over my consciousness more than any other place in the galaxy when I awoke. That snapshot on the space-time continuum implanted the emotions which I began to swallow—or perhaps choke—down every day.

The hangar, shrouded by misuse over the decades, stood bare with each launchpad, scrapped of any reminders of past machinations. But I had forgotten every detail of it. That is, until Max arrived.

Our cells bordered one another, but time separated the many isolated days following my renaissance and Max's arrival. He came—as I came, I suppose—wrapped in cloth and wearing crudely fashioned garments. Here was a reflection of my appearance. We both displayed unkemptness, hunger, and fear, but through communication with this seeming doppelganger, my memory scored a victory.

Maximilian Robertson, as I would find his name to be, had an air of demonic ether far more potent than mine, yet his tone clearly showed sanity and geniality. He lived his life as a serf until he was endowed by his own will with the skill of literacy in his teens.

As he grew, his wealth matured, mainly through his marriage into a money-blessed family. Through the newfound power of his family's status, he clambered aboard the half-sunk ship of politics.

Through my conversations with Max, the pantry of my memories was swept of its cobwebs and restored with a plethora of canned and dried goods. It was the spices from this pantry that gave me power—power to withdraw from my cell and make sense of the world.

Max reminded me of the cruel atmosphere in which we passed our previous years. Among these ecosystems, the marsh held the worst of them. The most loyal of these swamp-livers were snapping turtles. Their king overpowered the system, making a castle spire out of his minions and placing himself on the top.

But most people in the nation viewed this crooked reptile differently: he was their leader. President Mikhail Stena lived, like all the others, in his mansion at the heart of Atlanta. I had lived my life in Columbia, as I began to recall, ten miles from where land met the rising tide.

It had the best geography, out of all the seaboard cities, for the location of the US Space Initiative's hangar. On the other hand, by the time of my capture, no helmet, glove, or oxygen mask had made contact with it for decades, or so the tale had gone. But a citizen's knowledge proved to be the deadliest of my pantry's contents; I had stored it carefully, and Stena's men would have to pry the door off to find it.

* * *

It was a balmy morning in my early adulthood when I first met Max. Max, at 20 years my senior, had already begun his political career. I worked at the hangar as a test pilot then. My vessels had the average height of 22 of me stacked on one another's heads. Their divine bodies allowed them to explore the cosmos with more efficiency and agility than any previous space agencies' vessels. Just two moons prior to that morning, Stena sent an ultimatum to advance our current vessel system. These new beasts could carry thrice that of previous loads and complete travel between

Earth and moon in mere hours, with "great stealth." Everyone rejoiced. No one saw confusion.

But on that morning, we had just completed this set of vessels when a Stena gang, led by Max, apprehended my crew with a different Atlanta decree—a *very* different one. It specified that the nation's debt had grown to the point that the ship had sunk, and our agency and its projects were to be scrapped. Max suggested a new working position within the Air Force to compensate for my troubles and sent me to Western Tennessee for the opportunity—as far away from the hangar as Stena could push me.

Max, meanwhile, curled up inside Stena's regime, happily employed, and completing any project that occupied his days. But by the time of his conviction, he had sleepwalked throughout the government for so long that curiosity overcame him. His crime resembled my own, but from a higher perspective.

Stena never bothered to clean Max's storage of memories, and my pantry's replenishment alluded to escape from Stena's imprisonment. To our dissatisfaction, the only option for our departure became very audible. Stena's cronies, however, would not hear the slamming of doors, even under their noses.

Thus, we concurred to leave on the largest celebratory day of the year: Stena's birthday. Each office or structure would hold a party for President Stena. It was just a week away, and we knew that our guards and every government official in the prison would be making preparations for Stena's birthday tour of government offices. The easiest way to slip out, Max informed me, would be to take advantage of Max's hidden, government-issued bio-tattoo, imprinted to his scalp, shrouded with hair. The tattoo, unbeknownst to the guards (and to Max until a few days before when his memory had surfaced), would allow him to gain access to any door, including a locked supply closet in the back of his cell.

On Stena's birthday, after all the guards had gone to prepare the building for their benevolent czar's visit, Max began pacing his cell, attempting to look more contemplative than operative. He began circling around his supply closet, then pulled his head lower and scratched his head until finally an audible click pierced the room, and he drew the door open.

Max knew of air ducts—found solely in these closets—that spanned the entire prison in a circuit design. Climbing the shelf inside the closet he reached out at the duct and slowly pried the cover off. I heard him shuffle as he wound himself into the opening and into the chamber. Slithering into the duct, he next found the duct inside my closet, dropped into it, unlocked it, and allowed me to follow his plan through the tunnels far above the heads of government officials, clamoring through metal appliances with metallic bangs and squeaks.

After snaking for countless hours, we discovered our exit in the Office of Prisoner Possessions. Just as we expected, the office was deserted, and its entrance—as far as the employees knew—was locked. Stored inside a file among the office possessions were the clothes I once owned and a curious object which I had no recollection of having. The object, a brass key with an inscribed message, could only unlock one area, if I truly had possession of it: Ghost-town. Engraved into the key was the message *FOR CHILDREN'S USE ONLY.* Though it confused us both, we decided to pursue the question later.

In the hallway outside the office, to our amazement, not a person could be seen. We raced down it and found a set of doors, which we unlocked with Max's head, and entered into the perpendicular hall. From there, we jogged past rooms to the building's exit, walking through the outlet without an eye falling on us.

We discovered that the prison was situated on a river-bent peninsula. After visiting a nearby train station, we located ourselves on the map, in the foothills of the Smokies and the docks of the Tennessee River: the outskirts of Knoxville. Using a credit card I found inside my coat, we bought two tickets for a trip to Atlanta, a city we had no intent of traveling to. Hence, we discarded these tickets—their sole purpose was to provide a destination to give to Stena's men once they began investigating our escape. We both understood that only one real destination would lead us to revenge on Stena's regime: Columbia, SC.

With our tickets in hand—bought with cash, of course—Max and I, with changed appearances, boarded a robot-operated train. As we raced down the track to the east, I could only constantly wander back to my days spent pacing around the launchpads. The last operation that Stena had given us, Project Fast Fox (or PFF), gave us hundreds of rocketry vessels. As I understood, they all lay in disarray, standing on their platforms, waiting for someone to cut the knot in the strings holding them to the Earth, allowing them to fly away. In the meantime, gravity continued to clench them with a cosmic grasp, keeping them keenly weighed to the Earth.

When the mountains began to roll out and the Divine Dough Roller negated the differences in topography, there was no doubt that we were reaching Columbia and that the distance would narrow quickly now. As the Eastern Seaboard came into view, my eyes grew an affinity toward the mountainous structure before me: the hangar. The train lurched suddenly, changing course toward the center of the blackened city—a city with towering buildings but hardly any light within to wake the city from its slumber.

The train hissed as it retired its propulsion and began to decelerate. Meanwhile, I sat with my face to the window, staring into the lukewarm night, watching for any activity. Then, just as we could begin to read the signs surrounding the station, along one platform, a man—one with a very serious complexion and stature— made his way through the bustling folk. It appeared that the stranger might really be no stranger, for we had most likely seen him before. But as the train came near to a halt, pacing at a few miles an hour, I noticed that he seemed to be waiting for this disembarking train. As I became more concerned, I looked about, and recognized that since Columbia was near the end of the line, hardly any passengers remained. My concern grew. The likelihood neared zero that this stranger, wearing the insignia of Stena's establishment, was waiting to do business with any person besides Max or me. We wanted no business with this stranger.

I felt every muscle in my body tense to dart away from the stranger, toward the rear of the train, and continue our hiding. But, at this point, we understood that our suspiciousness would never lift with such a move. Thus, we chose to exit the train, as any other would, with increasing caution to escape from this fellow's presence as quickly as possible.

To our dismay, we were immediately apprehended upon exiting our car.

"'Ello. My name should be of no use to you," the man related with a bit of a Slovak dialect, "but if either wish to continue your journey, it is best for you to follow me."

That last bit was as good a reason as ever to attempt our escape, but to no avail. He did not attempt to chain us or detain us in any manner as I expected, but he produced two other agents. The three of them surrounded us to block our path. As we walked, I began to notice a lanyard that hung out of the stranger's pocket—a government-issued ID of sorts, I figured. I followed, forced by Stena's agents, but also planning to rob that ID from the stranger, if I could only escape.

Hence, when one man was mildly distracted by a cell phone call, Max, having a shared mindset, sent his torso into this man's side with enough brute force to throw the man off balance, forcing his phone from his ear to the other side of the street. Meanwhile, I wasted no time in toppling over the stranger, who was standing on my opposite side. Finally, just as I saw the third man pull a device from his blazer, I took the moment to reach deep into the stranger's pocket and rummaged to find his ID. The man managed to retrieve the device and point it at Max: the last time I would hear his voice.

The last word I remember from Max was "Please!" Then, a piercing noise hit the air—a tasing device. Meanwhile, I sprinted down the block. As I stole glances at the ID, I read that the man was indeed a crony of Stena's with the name of Ilyich Legig. It seemed that his whole responsibility was to silence any word spoken regarding the hangar. At that time, I was stricken with confusion. Why would any government personnel be concerned with the secrecy of an unused government facility? The largest feeling that rang through my body was the need to answer that question, but I could only do such a thing by entering the hangar.

When I reached the hangar doors, thinking that I could open them with Legig's identification card, I immediately tried to pierce the security system with the card, fearing that some companion camera was watching to match the face with the card. It finally pinged with a point of green light: the most glorious green speck for me in countless days of isolation from the launch-yard. I yanked the door open and raced into oblivion, as I realized that the entire building was pitch black.

Groping the wall, I found a light switch, which illuminated the room enough so that I found the door that I needed. This door appeared with a shining knob and the appearance of use—recent use.

Stunned by the apprehension that the hangar might be in use, I widened the door's gap, allowing for light to appear in the doorway as the sun first began to appear over the horizon. As the light struck the platforms, I became bewildered that, though a few rockets were secured to the hangar, just as many seemed to have disappeared.

Struck by this realization, I began inspecting each rocket. I meandered among them, examining each one for signs of operation. I found a few—enough to know that they still had commission. *But for what?* was the question, and I felt destined to discover the answer as I became convinced that the entire scheme was a plot against our society by the Stena administration. Finally, I jammed "my" ID into the slot for identification accreditation at the base of a rocket I remembered once testing—the first "Fast Fox" rocket to be constructed and tested. I concluded, with that action, that I was sealing destiny: I was to travel aboard the rocket.

After settling into its main compartment, I found all the controls, put on a colleague's old space suit still left in the craft, and prepared to defy gravity. Finally, I was minutes away from taking another great journey. I had no idea as to the destination until I found a control center with a "control history" application: the last flight descended back to Earth from the moon just two months ago, and it took just 30 minutes. Prepared for one of my fastest tests yet, I determined to make one small step onto our lone natural satellite.

It took just 10 minutes to leave Earth's atmosphere, a third of the way into the trip, with nearly unbearable turbulence. Yet, I managed to forget it, my eyes and thoughts keenly focused on what to expect once I arrived. I discovered through the control history that my landing spot would not be at just any location. It would be the Gagarin Lunar Cosmodrome: a launching and arrival area for rockets exiting and entering the moon.

Twenty minutes later, what remained of the rocket— the compartment I still inhabited—made impact upon the surface of the Cosmodrome. The turbulence had deteriorated my skull and my brain to mush. Meanwhile, workers at the Cosmodrome, appearing to be no more than 16 years old, raced to my ship to find the traveler of the unexpected flight.

* * *

When I had regained composure enough to sit in my hospital bed, I attempted to figure out my environment. Again, many of the storage jars in my pantry had expired and I had hardly any recollections of my escape or journey through the cosmos. In the end, once the drugs had given me strength to at least speak and understand my external contexts, the Director of the Cosmodrome—the eldest of its inhabitants at 17 years of age—came to brief me on all the information that had evaded me.

It was he, Director Eric Mend, who replaced my expired stock. He informed me of many predicaments, especially those political in nature, with regard to the Stena regime. Stena had wanted this group of teens to have flight access to the moon, and he had a purpose. The over-archer towered above: He wanted these children, essentially, to mine for all the materials of lunar landscape. He wanted to enrich himself through this effort, but it would also slow the Earth's tides, as the moon became more nonexistent. His hopes enumerated, he thought this deceleration of the tides might also reduce coastal flooding.

All the while, he wanted it secret. This, simply, had the effect of not allowing anyone to escape his regime if they gained access to his vessels. Thus were the wishes of our president, but I had just landed upon his treasure. My pantry quickly restored itself; my story never ended. And my pantry had just transformed into a store.

Trevor Wendt's "A Wall Between Worlds" won First Place for Fiction in the Grade 11-12 category.

In Remembrance of You by Hollie Cassandra Powless

You may not remember the shift in my stance, as the bright
    smile on my young face disappeared.

That day you said those words was not the same for me as it
    was for you.

To you it was just a stupid comeback, something you said
    without thinking.

But to me, it was everything, it became my whole world.

You were the start of this introverted girl, shoving me into a
    shell of sadness and despair.

You poked fun at my differences, my clothes, and how I was
    heavier than you.

You made me feel less than my best, less than who I was.

You stepped on my fragile young brain and planted self-hatred
    into my heart.

I hadn't known I was different, I hadn't know we weren't the
    same.

You kept watering that seed in my chest, making it grow into a
    never-ending black hole of confusion and compulsion.

You started my habits of nail picking, lip chewing, cheek
    biting, and of being afraid to be me.

When you stopped feeding the ever-aching pit in my soul, the
    pain did not just go away.

Others kept it alive by calling me names, by treating me like a
    wad of gum stuck to the bottom of their name brand
    sneakers.

You made me realize my differences.

You took my smile away.

The seed may not be growing, but it is still ever there.

It stays in the remembrance of you.

Hollie Cassandra Powless's "In Remembrance of You" won Second Prize for Poetry in the Grade 9-10 category.

Hidden by the Stars by Kylie Cox

Five years before:

Every time a person dies, a star is born. Every dream, unfinished or complete, is their light. Dreamers forever shine bright. Dream on dear child, for you are the brightest star.

Present:

From above the old stone orphanage you can see the shape of a girl, curled against the chimney on the darkened roof. Beside her is a small candle, the light dim, dancing. She pulls an ancient book from the ratted pocket of her dress. Then, she blows out the candle and gazes up. Every night you will find her staring at the stars and reading her book. And if you listen carefully in the dark, you can hear her small voice whisper into the night. *Serenity.* She is the one. She is the star.

Bravery:

I've followed her since she was brought here. Since her mother died and her father left. I've seen her grow but she's never seen me. Only in her dreams. She calls me Dream Wolf to her friends. She isn't wrong, but she isn't right. She knows so little, but she's beginning to grow. Soon, I will show her everything. But for now, I think it's appropriate that we meet.

In the night, when the other children have gone to bed, Serenity stares at the fake, glowing stars on the ceiling. She stares at these as much as she gazes at the real ones. She is connected to the stars more than she will ever realize. She finally curls into the blankets. And that is when I go in.

"Serenity," I whisper into the dark. She sits up and looks around. All she can see are the shadows bouncing on the wall, including the shape of a wolf. Her eyes grow wide as she sees my shadow move along the wall, stalking back and forth. She is definitely scared, but also curious. The girl climbs out of bed to try and get to me, but I growl, and she stays back. She can't get close. I know she is scared of me now, but her curiosity grows. And then she begins to speak.

Serenity:

I stay up late again. I like it when it gets dark and the fake stars glow above my bed. I arrange them into constellations and pictures. I'm drawn to them. But as I lay back, a voice calls out my name. In the dark, a wolf shadow dances along the wall. It takes shape, and soon, it is real. The wolf is dark with black fur the color of midnight. A stark white muzzle stands out against his dark body and a pale symbol occupies his forehead. A slate grey crescent. I move to see him, but he growls. I want to scream, but I don't. He watches me with piercing gold eyes, drawing me in. I am too scared to run, rooted where I sit. So I say hello.

Bravery:

Every night I stalk back and forth. Some nights, she says, "Hello, Mr. Wolf." Some nights, she tells me everything that happened that day. And occasionally, she yawns and waves, too tired to speak. Every night I listen to her soft voice. I never speak, although I can. I never let her get close. The patience is something I'm used to, but I'm beginning to yearn for my home. I was desperate when I started to look for her, but she is too young. She will not be willing. I'm so homesick it hurts in my chest, but she is the only way back, so I must wait.

I start to stay in the shadows, leaving her be. She is so young; she isn't ready. Serenity tries to find me, but I stay hidden. She calls out to me, but I'm a silent watcher. After a few nights, she stops trying. Tonight, she looks so sadly toward me, though she cannot see me. I feel guilt in my chest, but I have to forget it. It's odd, though. Never have I ever felt guilty about anything, and here is a child, no more than 10, causing me more emotion than I've ever experienced. I was only meant for darkness and loneliness, but I've felt different things inside me. Bright, happy things. It's so confusing. Maybe she's worth it.

As I watch from the shadows, she gathers her book and clambers out the window. She gracefully edges up the ladder outside her window up onto the roof. She doesn't wake the others as she climbs, and it is almost like she is a shadow, like me, moving silently through the night. I follow her onto the roof, but stay hidden. I watch her as she settles under the stars. Then, she does something surprising, something I didn't think she would ever understand. She turns her shining eyes to the stars. Waving her hand to signal hello, she calls out her welcome.

"Hi, Mama."

In that moment, something changes inside me. Tears well in my eyes as I remember my own home, my own family, that I can't get back to. But maybe there's a chance. Serenity has lost her mother, much like I lost mine when I was young. I don't have to wait any longer. She deserves to know. I owe that to her. So I creep toward her, pressed against the darkness. Then, in a whisper of wind, I appear. No longer am I a shadow, nor a wolf. When Serenity turns around, I see the surprise spread across her face. She doesn't see a wolf. She sees a boy. She sees me.

Serenity:

   I hear rustling behind me. My heart beats like drums in my chest. What if someone has followed me? What if they know? I turn slowly to see what the sound is, and I swear my eyes almost pop out of my head. Behind me is not a child or even the imaginary wolf. Behind me stands a teenage boy.

   He is tall and pale with a lithe frame. His hair is darker than the night, dark as pitch. He almost appears normal to me, but there is something unsettling about this boy. His eyes are the color of autumn, of amber. They are gold as a full moon and stand in great contrast to his handsome face. And barely visible on his pale skin is the faint trace of a crescent shaped scar in the middle of his forehead. Just like the wolf.

   I want to scream, but instead I gaze in awe. He towers over me, his piercing stare burning into my skin. I match his look, getting drawn into his shining eyes. He seems to relax, and I can see a faint smile appear on his lips. I smile wide and he matches me, showing pearly white teeth and canines, just slightly too large for his mouth. I know it is him. I muster up my courage, and finally, finding my voice, I call out to the boy.

   "Hello again, Mr. Wolf. Where have you been?"

Bravery:

   I startle a bit when she speaks. Her voice isn't scared. It's quiet but filled with courage and laced with curiosity. I slowly walk toward her, wobbly on two long legs.

   "Can I sit?" I ask her.

   My voice is low and carries through the night.

She nods and pats the ground beside her. Her pale green eyes are wide as saucers as she gazes at me. She is truly pretty. Chestnut hair flows lightly over her shoulders and spills onto a white nightgown. Her brown skin appears to sparkle in the pale moonlight. She sits in complete serenity. Her name fits her well.

"My name's Bravery," I tell her.

"Oh," she whispers. "Mine is —"

"Serenity. I know," I interrupt. "What are you doing out here this late?"

"I'm visiting Mama and her friends," she says. "Mama always wanted to be a star. She told me," she whispers, showing me the writing in her book. It's her mother's handwriting. Guilt claws up my throat when I see it, but I keep it down.

"I knew your mother," I tell her. Her attention snaps to my eyes. I feel myself blush a little as she watches me expectantly. "Your mother and I were best friends. I was there when you were born. When she ..." I'm unable to finish.

She nods. I can see the confusion in her doe eyes, but she keeps quiet. After a moment, she slips her tiny hand into mine. I almost flinch, but it's comforting instead. I stare at our hands, the way her darker skin contrasts mine. She smiles weakly at me. We sit in silence for a while and Serenity offers comfort, silent and sweet. She is so much like her mother.

Alexandria. I miss her everyday. She was so curious and beautiful and I loved her. She was never like the other people. The others feared death, but Alexandria welcomed it, challenged it. She had dreams brighter than most. I couldn't bring myself to sacrifice her. Instead when she passed away, I took her soul and joined it to my family.

I am the constellation Canis Major and my family is the stars within me. I've been alive for centuries, living off sacrifices. The souls of dreamers keep me alive and keep the stars aligned. But Alexandria was so bright and I loved her too much to purely use her. She became one of my stars, always with me.

Serenity *is* Alexandria, but even brighter. She has more dreams and wishes. She isn't afraid. She never will be. She is kinder and more curious than her mother, something I thought I'd never see in another person. And she's suffering, confined in the orphanage like a caged bird. I'm going to help her spread her wings and soar above all others. It's the least I can do.

I'm not going to tell her everything tonight. It's too much to take. So we mostly sit in silence, with Serenity occasionally pointing out the constellations I know by heart. And as the sun starts to peek around the corner of the horizon, I stand to leave.

"Don't go!" she calls. Her eyes plead and I feel so guilty leaving her.

"I must go. But I will return tonight and I will tell you everything," I promise.

She nods and watches as a shadow replaces my being. Then, she leaves and crawls back through her window and into bed. And though she doesn't know it, after her breathing becomes soft and steady, I stand watch over her. I watch her tiny chest rise and fall in time with the world, and my heart swells. I kiss her forehead softly as I leave, a brush of warmth in the darkness. This girl is taking my heart and she doesn't even know it yet.

* * *

We meet like that every night. I tell her everything. I tell her bits of the story each night, like chapters from a book. She is wise beyond her age. She understands me and doesn't think anything is fake. Our trust grows, too. At first she keeps lots of distance between us, afraid she will touch me and I'll explode into a cloud of smoke. Tonight, she grabs me by the arm and pulls me excitedly to our spot. We whisper to each other through the night. She tells me about her friends and schoolwork. She shows me the sketches she's been drawing. She likes to draw me and tonight she shows me a picture of me as a wolf howling beside her, her arms wrapped around me and her face huddled into my fur. She's really artistic. And beautiful.

Now the sun crests over the city, casting a reddish glow over us. Serenity is curled against my side and my arm is around her. Her breathing is slow and rhythmic as she sleeps. The sun makes her hair appear gold in the sunlight. Her green eyes sparkle in the new light. Gently, I lift her into my arms and carry her to bed. I lightly tuck her in, careful not to wake her. I gaze out over the rows of beds inside the orphanage. It almost surprises me how dull the other children are. They are black and white, and then I look back at Serenity. She glows green and yellow and blue and violet. She really does outshine the rest. And I cannot believe she is almost mine. I leave her silently, slowly beginning the agonizing wait until I see my friend again.

* * *

I have no recollection of ever being scared before. Now I know why humans fear it. Over the next few days, Serenity never comes to see me. She falls ill and spends her days in bed. I try to visit, but people are in and out with her. Doctors visit daily, checking her pulse and temperature. I can feel her growing weaker. But that's impossible! She can't be dying. Can she?

Serenity's eyes roll in her sleep. I sit by her side for hours, and she isn't getting better. Her skin is pale as the moon and her forehead shines with fever. She is so weak, the flame of her life barely a flicker. Her tiny hand in mine is so frail. So this is death. This is true pain. Serenity will not survive the night. Only a few more hours with her at best. But she will fight to the end. She has always fought. I whisper her name to her. Her fingers curl around my thumb, desperately holding on. Her eyes flutter open. Her green eyes hold everything that is her. And they hold an unbeatable pain. Fear.

Serenity:

I know I'm sick. I'm dying. The doctors say my heart is sick. Dying hurts a lot more than the books and movies show. In the fog of the fever, I hear my name. It's far away, but I finally snap myself to focus. The first thing I see is gold. Bravery is here. He's the reason I've fought. He is my only friend and the only family I have left. I can't abandon him. I can't lose him.

My limbs are leaden with sickness. Everything hurts, but Bravery is here. He will heal me.

"Bravery," my voice cracks. His eyes widen. He looks scared. "I'm gonna die."

"Yes." He hesitates before saying this. He doesn't want me to know. But he knows I'm smarter than that.

"Can you save me?" I can see him flinching away.

"No, I can't. I …" His voice shatters. "I couldn't save your mother either." Tears well in his eyes, making the gold shimmer.

I wish I could go back to sleep. "Mama's a star," I whisper.

He nods, and a tear drops over his porcelain skin. It hurts to move, but I reach up and catch it in my palm.

"Make me a star."

I hear his breath hitch. He looks like the idea hurts him. There's something he didn't tell me yet.

"I can't do that to you," he breathes, barely audible. His voice is low, a growl. It's uncertainty that's frightening.

"But why? You made Mama a star. Why can't I be a star?" My voice is weak, but demanding.

"I don't want to hurt you!" Bravery snaps. His burst of anger scares me, and I cringe away. The hardness in his eyes disappears when he realizes what he has done.

"I'm sorry, Serenity. I can't make you a star."

"Tell me why."

"Because," he starts, "I would have to kill you. In order to make you a star, I would have to kill you by my own hand. I love you, Serenity. I would never forgive myself."

I'm speechless. He killed Mama. Or at least finished her. But I'm not angry. I'm not sad. This is what I want.

My voice is as clear as I can make it. "Bravery, I have nothing left. You are the world to me. If it means you have to kill me for us to be together, then so be …" I gasp. My chest is pierced by an invisible knife.

Bravery reaches for me in alarm. We both know my time is up. It's now or never.

I hear his voice right before I fade into sleep.

"I'll make you a star, Serenity. And you'll be the brightest there ever was."

Bravery:

I hold her in my arms when she dies. I pull her last breath away and watch as the green fire burns out in her eyes. And I cry. I cry for Alexandria, for my loss of humanity so many years ago. And I cry for Serenity, the person I love most in this world.

Now I sit on the edge of her bed, her pale body limp in my arms. I'm not finished. I made a promise I intend to keep.

I pull her soul from the depths of her heart. It is bright green, almost too bright to behold. I hold it in my hand, take one last look at Serenity's body, and disappear into the sky. In my true form, I place her in my constellation. She will be Sirius, the brightest star in Canis Major. Forevermore she will shine bright and guide the people she was once a part of. And forever, she will be with me.

Epilogue:

I stand on the edge of a dark roof. The night is chilly and quiet. A flurry of wind erupts beside me. There stands a panther, sleek and dark. Her eyes sparkle bright green. Serenity. She changes into herself, now a teen. She's as graceful as the animal she has chosen to become. She looks at me and smiles, and the cold washes away. She holds out her hand, beckoning into the night. And I take it.

Kylie Cox's "Hidden by the Stars" won Second Prize for Fiction in the Grade 7-8 category.

Like Hungry Dogs by Lily Griffioen

I fall further and further into myself
I feel the darkness all around
And as I curl up in the cold abyss, I can see them

The arms come reaching down for me
Their skin tattooed, soft and light, with words of comfort and
        concern
"Are you okay?" "What's wrong?" "I'm here for you"

My mind screams, begging for me to reach up
To take their hands and wrap them around me
To smother myself in the calm glow of concern

I want nothing more than to apologize, to tell them that I'm
        sorry
I'm sorry that I lied to you
Because I am not okay, and I am not just tired, and it has not
        just been a long day

But I can't because even though the words sit in my mouth like
        hungry dogs
Pushing and scratching to be free
The shield of deceit is all too familiar

Its handles worn from use, grooves formed from my relentless
        grip
The front carved with lies
And words of false hope

It's cracked though

The hands are becoming stronger
And me?

I'm becoming weaker

Lily Griffioen's "Like Hungry Dogs" won Second Prize for Poetry in the Grade 11-12 category.

End of Times by Faith Sweet

For any other person, the sand that danced around the beach in whisps would have stung her bare skin. For the woman who stood before the salty ocean, the sand seemed to curve around her as if some force was willing it not to touch her golden brown skin. Each wave that crashed down into the wet earth seemed prone to flow around her exposed feet. The sand and the wind and the waves and all of life knew she was not to be touched.

With a wildflower crown atop her head and gown that seemed to be made out of the yellow light from a thousand fireflies, the forces of nature bowed at her feet. She was the creator, the mother of all life that flourished on her green little planet. In her presence, you forgot all of your insignificance. Her golden gaze could seduce the bravest men and the strongest women.

Alas, within all her grace and power hid a curse—a burden shackled to her mind. She loved too much, and on the stormy beach where she stood was a man whom she loved above all she had created. He was the man who was feared by everything light had touched. When she whispered his name, it was swept up with the dancing sand and blown out to sea, only heard by the lonely sailors who were anchored to the ocean floor. She held enough love in her heart to make up for all the hate thrown into his.

He could feel every living organism's fear of his being. Every soul he collected burdened him with more blood on his hands. He knew that in his presence, the ground shivered and the light faded. With his arms laced with barbed wire and a gloved hand that held a scythe dipped in crimson, he knew. All the dread forced into his very being took its toll. He was so broken that he could never love.

He was the Reaper and she was Mother Earth. It was Life and Death together in unison. She was his only driving force, for without Life there was no Death. In the moments they harbored on the stormy beach, the beloved goddess of life succumbed to her love for the angel of death. No feeling could ever pass through them—their physical forms had been shed long ago, but when their eyes locked a forest fire ignited, a wave dragged a city out to sea, a volcano spit sputtering magma, destroying a silent village.

The rhythmic thud of every heartbeat on earth sounded like the drums of a great king's marching band as she sailed toward him. It was the screams of the souls damned to hell that pierced her melodic rhythm. Unity could only last for mere seconds in their presence.

Nothing could delay their sacred work. It was deemed too important by the grace of opposing forces, a force that had to be obeyed. Souls were collected, years passed in the blink of an eye, souls were replenished.

Throughout their eternity, there was always one thing that was evident above all else. The push and pull of their powers were far from equal. In their silent agreement, Death must always bow to Life's roaring lioness of mastery. The toll the Reaper accepted drove his spite to morph into a wicked plan.

Day by day, the grand Reaper's malice steadily rose. His lust for power pushed heavily against the thin line that separated his concept of good and evil. The king of mortal ends dared to defy the only ideals he and the goddess of light had to follow. He lusted for the moment his ashen hand could lunge for the beloved throat of Life. For he was the four horsemen, he was the seven deadly sins, he was the mutilated king of hell.

In his greed and vile coveting, he took to the skies, working to deceive the rightful heir to a throne of empowerment. Mother Earth's downfall came swiftly, and all in her desire to love and be loved. She fell down, down into the darkness that enthralled her veil of vitality. Skeleton arms and shrieking faces devoured her glowing soul, and death rose up in her time of absence. A year of torment was bestowed upon all of the glorious creatures that filled her heart.

The dead spirits of all those once living endlessly slaved for him. Every beautiful life was crushed under the weight of Death's cold avail. Darkness was alive in his presence. Terror choked the air out of everybody his dead eyes gazed upon—all except one. Even with all of his wrongdoing, Mother Earth's heart still beat with her love for him.

Her pleas and cries brought her no mercy in the darkness she was chained to. Her grace was spent. Cowering under the knife held against her heart by the only one with enough power to do so, she wept for every shell of a soul her counterpart struck down. Her Majesty was gone.

The forces of existence's wandering eye did not overlook the bleak corruption. They roared that Death's vengeance would be his own end.

The endless nights that followed were filled with the sounds of fulfilled suffering. It was only when every being had lost hope in the salvation of their Mother Earth that silence struck down upon the land. No screaming souls called out, no vengeful demons roared. The darkness stood still. All of the fear had been taken, all emotion was gone. On the very edge of a breath, calm.

Every entity stood frozen as from the ashes of swelling darkness rose the haunting sound of violin strings being strung by a ghostly bow. The end had come. The Reaper's violin sang for the loss of the only force who loved him. Its music shuddered across the desolate land that once was home to all that was good. In pure, wholesome affliction, Death itself danced for his love, his driving force. Without Life, there was no Death, there was no existence, there was no tale to tell.

Slowly, each and every soul he himself had damned rose to dance in mourning for their lost goddess. Bearing the weight of loss for thousands of organisms, Death played his beautiful tune in sorrowful regret. He wept in silence for all that he had caused. The grand master of death could not love, but alas he could feel. What woes were held were merely mortal now. The sole creator of all that ever had walked the now broken earth was gone. The green little home that once flourished now sat only in hazy memories.

The end of time had closed the exact moment it had opened. In the deep grief shared by all of the wandering souls, no one could bow to Death's will. There was no power left for him to consume. He was defeated. At once, he was no more an immortal being with forbidden power. All he had become was an entity with a violin.

So with the lullaby's final notes, he sang his queen to sleep, pleading with the Almighty for forgiveness as the world shattered around him.

Faith Sweet's "End of Times" won First Prize for Fiction in the Grade 9-10 category.

The Pine Trees by Abbey Churney

The pines trees line the driveway.

There is no avoiding their presence as I stroll up the long path
of dirt.

I look up at them, in their long rows and large numbers, their
many branches and rough bark

And notice how much smaller I am compared to them.

But I know the truth.

The pine trees are fading.

Just last week, one collapsed. Its remains still lay in the
pasture, towered over by those who will follow,
someday.

The pine needles, usually ever so hardy, have been plucked
from the tops of certain trees.

Death's slow harvest has begun.

It's more noticeable when the wind blows.

As the weakening branches thrash and flail, you wonder how
much it will take for them to snap—

For the roots to unearth.

For the crash, as trunk and branches meet the soil for the
second and last time in life.

The night makes it worse.

Only hearing the roar as wind and branches meet

Leaves the mind to wander.

What is happening?

The darkness holds no confirmation nor consolation.
I let the worry consume me until another topic claims my
          thoughts and sleep finds me
Worn out from its long journey.

And then morning comes.
I gaze out from the window, witnessing the rebirth of the day.
Grass glitters with the golden light that has fallen over the
          world.
Birds sing.
The horses meander throughout the corral, nibbling at hay and
          testing each other's boundaries.
The mug of tea, a shade of gold darker than the sunlight,
          warms my fingers.

Everything is normal.

As the too-sweet liquid flows down my throat, I notice the
          fallen pine on the drive.

I really must learn to embrace the dark.

*Abbey Churney's "The Pine Trees" won First Prize for Poetry
in the Grade 11-12 category.*

Author & Artist Biographies

The cover artist and authors were invited to write short biographies of themselves.

Ever since **Ashlyn Bottger** was a little girl, she loved to draw. Some of her favorite things to do are practice drawing, play the saxophone, go to the beach, run cross country, and hang out with her friends. She is currently 14 years old and will be a freshman at Paw Paw High School in the fall. She has always lived in Paw Paw, Michigan, with her dad, her mom, her older brother Sam, and her younger brother Will.

William "Anthony" Bradley is an eighth grader at Paw Paw Middle School. In addition to being a first time award-winning poet, Anthony is an honor roll student, starting football player, and state champion wrestler. When not watching Flowrestling videos or playing his Xbox, Anthony enjoys spending time with his parents and his four sisters.

Abbey Churney was probably up before you, and will probably go to sleep later than you as well. When she's not engaged in her extensive battle with sleep, she tries to find time to spend with those she cares for (including—but not limited to—her family, friends, and horse), as well as time to write ideas for stories she rarely seems to complete and time to attempt playing the violin. She enjoys drinking her too-sweet tea on a near daily basis (preferably with a cat for company) and is probably still trying to predict what will happen in the *Infinity War* sequel.

Rowan Clark is a poet, songwriter, and performer who grew up in the small beach town of South Haven, Michigan. His "day job" is to be an eighth grader at Upton Middle School. Rowan's most treasured performance to date is playing the role of Jem in the Twin City Players production of *To Kill a Mockingbird*. He has a love for satirical humor (obsessed with Dilbert and Calvin and Hobbes). Rowan's passions are dystopian novels, playing soccer, and spending time outdoors, interacting with the forces of nature. His inspiration for his poem "Searing Cold" came from climbing trees in the winter wonderland of Southwest Michigan. He frequently acquires ideas about his artistic endeavors through his interactions with nature.

Kylie Cox is an eighth grader at Paw Paw Middle School. She loves school and playing soccer, along with reading and writing. Kylie is imaginative and very outgoing. When she's not on the field or hanging out with friends, you can find her curled up with a new book or drawing simple sketches. She enjoys jotting down her stories and is often inspired by her close friends. One of her biggest dreams is to have her writings published and sold across the country for young adults to enjoy. She plans to continue writing in the future, because she wants to share her ideas with the world through her words and through her stories.

Penny Duran is a global citizen and calls Houston, Texas home. As a child in a diplomatic family, she has grown up overseas in Egypt, Germany, New Zealand, the Philippines, and Poland. She is educated in the German school system and enjoys writing in English and German. Her works have received recognition in Australia, Austria, Canada, Germany, Poland, and the United States. Life with little sister Lillian (who is by no means ever a clueless chicken) provides inspiration for Penny's stories. Together they share a passion for dancing, having performed in ballet productions of *Giselle*, the *Nutcracker*, *Sleeping Beauty*, and the *Wayward Daughter*.

Renee Elrod has submitted works in the Van Buren County Teen Creative Writing Challenge since seventh grade. This is her first year competing as a high schooler. Her inspirations are her books, her family, and her friends. She enjoys reading novels in her spare time as an escape from reality. Partaking in this Challenge is always fun for her and she enjoys doing it every year.

Ilona Fiedorowicz is 13 years old and lives in South Haven, where she attends Baseline Middle School, part of South Haven Public Schools. She enjoys playing her cello, whose name is Perrin, and the piano (who is currently nameless). The Legend of Zelda is her number one video game series (and the only video games she really plays), and fantasy has been her ultimate obsession since kindergarten. Her favorite word is *usurper*, because, she says, "if you see that word in a book, something worth reading is happening." Her favorite color is blue, and her favorite animal is the red wolf. In her spare time, she reads fantasy, writes fantasy (all with swords), composes orchestral pieces, writes musicals, does karate, plays her instruments, personifies objects, plays Zelda, plays Dungeons and Dragons, eats chocolate, and watches sitcoms. She may not want to be a full-time author when she grows up, but she does know that she will be writing stories for the rest of her life.

Miriam K. Gartland is a 14-year-old budding author, hoping to make a splash in the ocean that is published fiction. When she is not working on her most recent novel in progress, she can be found drawing, drinking multiple cups of tea, reading interesting novels, making frequent trips to the library, or quoting lines from her favorite books and movies.

Lily Griffioen is a graduating senior at Portage Northern High School. This is her second year entering the Challenge. In 2017, Lily won First Prize in Grade 11-12 for her poem "A nervous disorder characterized by a state of uneasiness and apprehension."

Maliah Lewnfield is completing her freshman year at Paw Paw High School. This is her first year entering the Challenge.

Sarah Mayfield is an eighth grader at Paw Paw Middle School. This is her first year entering the Challenge.

Luz Moreno is a graduating senior at Hartford High School. This is her first year entering the Challenge.

Hollie Cassandra Powless is a high school student. She enjoys singing in choir, performing in plays and musicals, and playing her saxophone in band. Hollie uses writing to express her thoughts and personal experiences. During the summer, she volunteers at a local youth camp as a counselor to children. Hollie currently resides in West Michigan.

Austin Riness says, "Born as the son of my father, being geeky was inevitable." At the age of two, he was able to log into a password-protected computer with ease. He inherited his compassion from his mother. His talent for writing came out of the woodworks. Up until the age of 16, he didn't understand why people wrote poetry. But he sees it now. There is beauty hidden behind the lawless world of poetry. Grammar is just a suggestion. Periods are an option. Passion is a must. The rhythm of the words and the depth of meaning that can be layered upon the page is truly awe-inspiring to him. He believes that poetry is one of the purest ways to release one's very soul for the world to see.

Faith Sweet has written short stories and poems since fourth grade and currently loves to write as a hobby. Her work was published in *The Poems That Ate Our Ears* in 2014. As a freshman, she took Writing and Lyrical Expression at Gobles High School. She plans to pursue a career in the arts.

Trevor Wendt, student of Mattawan High School, wishes to lend his skills on the computer to make a career as a joint-NASA employee and CIA operative, using his influence in both organizations and rallying those in a radical sector of the CIA to create a separate agency dedicated to the preservation of intergalactic peace through diplomacy between realms, which he and his future associates will name "the People in Gray" (PIG). His goals include negotiating with the super-bacteria colonies of Enceladus, colonizing Kepler 438b, and making peace accords between the Milky Way and Andromeda Galaxies to prevent a seemingly inevitable clash. In his free time, he plans to go to all dark recesses of the Earth to exterminate the Imperial measurement system and instill a new global measurement scheme based on an international system.

Eric Wheeler is a sophomore at Bangor High School. He has had a short story published in the 2017 Teen Writers Anthology and in the eBook Journey To Publication 2017 Anthology. Eric has two cats—Bonzi and Midnight—that love to bug him for attention while he is trying to write. He loves to bring happiness to others, whether it's by writing books or performing on the stage as an actor.

Judge Biographies

Melanie Dunbar is the editor of the Poetry Society of Michigan's journal, *Peninsula Poets*. Her poems can be found in *Gargoyle, Sweet: A Literary Confection, Clade Song,* and elsewhere. Her poem *daughterson* was a finalist in the 2017 Workhorse/Rabbit Catastrophe Press Real Good Poem Prize. She lives on a farm outside of Allegan with her family and their rooster, Mr. Beautiful.

Leslie Helakoski is the author, and sometimes illustrator, of 11 picture books including *Hoot & Honk Just Can't Sleep*—her newest release. Leslie's books, known for their humor and word play, include *Woolbur, Big Chickens, Big Chickens Fly the Coop, Fair Cow,* and *Big Pigs*. They have won acclaim with Junior Library Guild, received starred reviews, been highlighted in Book Sense Picks, and were nominated for awards in over 20 states across the country. She has illustrated her four most recent books, including *Doggone Feet!* (a best math choice by *Scholastic Magazine*). The upcoming *Ready or Not, Woolbur Goes to School* and *Are Your Stars Like My Stars* will be released in 2018 and 2019 respectively. She lives in Lawton, Michigan where she is a Regional Advisor for the Society of Children's Book Writers and Illustrators.

Elizabeth Kerlikowske published her first poem at 16, and she was hooked! She is the author of two full-length books, five chapbooks, and a children's book. Her poems and short short fictions appear in many journals, including *Barking Sycamores, Slab, Poesia, Poemeleon, New Verse News, Peacock Journal,* and others. Elizabeth was awarded the Community Medal for the Arts in 2017. Her work has been nominated for six Pushcart

Awards, but alas ... Elizabeth is president of Friends of Poetry, a 40+ year-old nonprofit dedicated to bringing people and poetry together. They are responsible for the Poems That Ate Our Ears contest for student writers. Elizabeth has three kids, twin grandsons, one husband, four cats, a PhD, and a lot to do.

Amy McInnis is a native of Michigan's Upper Peninsula. Her first book of poems, *Cut River*, was published in 2007 by Logan House Press, and her poems have been published in *Cimarron Review*, *CutBank*, *Mid-American Review*, and elsewhere. She teaches writing at Grand Valley State University and lives near Grand Rapids, Michigan.

Meghann Meeusen teaches children's and adolescent literature at Western Michigan University, where she works to develop innovative pedagogy approaches centering around the contextual nature of literature, as well as how individuals can become stronger critical thinkers through reading and research. She earned her PhD from Illinois State University, and she has recently published on children's adapted comics, young adult dystopia, and critical pedagogy approaches to adolescent literature. Her current research explores ideology and binary patterns in film adaptations of children's texts, and she has broader research interests in children's visual culture, gender studies in YA fantasy, and children's comics.

Janie Lynn Panagopoulos, Great Lakes author and historian, has worked in the field of historical research, interpretation, and writing for 38 years. Her books include the award-winning novels for young people *Traders in Time, Journey Back to Lumberjack Camp, Little Ship Under Full Sail,* and *A Faraway*

Home: An Orphan Train Story. She is currently working on her sixteenth book! Ms. Panagopoulos has won the prestigious Michigan Authors Award in addition to the Read Michigan Award, the Student Choice Award, and the Geographic Excellence in Media Award from the National Council for Geographic Education in Washington, D. C. Ms. Panagopoulos was also awarded a Content Service Provider's Honorable Mention Award for her videoconferencing and Distant Learning programs in writing and history. In her historical research, Ms. Panagopoulos has canoed over 4,000 miles on the Great Lakes following fur trade routes, studied with traditional Native American elders, participated in archaeological digs, and traveled by dog-sled, snowshoe, and wagon train. Today, she continues along the trails of history in search of our American/Great Lakes roots.

Elaine Stephens, educator and author, has spent her life sharing her love of reading and writing. Earning a Ph.D. from Michigan State University, she taught from preschool to graduate school. She was a professional development consultant and a university professor, receiving awards for excellence in teaching, leadership, and scholarship. Elaine has written numerous articles and co-authored 10 books on literacy, historical connections, and young adult literature. Her passion lies in encouraging and nurturing youth to become lifelong readers and writers. Elaine is an advocate for equity for women and girls and supports progressive endeavors. She has lived and worked in Michigan, New Jersey, and Taiwan and currently resides in South Haven.

Made in the USA
Columbia, SC
22 June 2018